TIES THAT BIND

GEORGE SMITH

SELECTED COLUMNS
FROM THE ANNISTON STAR

George Smith/Consolidated Publishing
Box 189
Anniston, AL 36202
www.annistonstar.com

Book Layout ©2015 BookDesignTemplates.com

Ordering Information:
Quantity sales. Special discounts are available on quantity purchases by corporations, associations, and others. For details, contact the "Special Sales Department" at the address above.

Ties That Bind / George Smith. -- 1st ed.
ISBN: 978-1519692771

To all the friends I've known

CONTENTS

THOSE WHO SERVED

FAITH

IN REMEMBRANCE

Introduction

I spent a lot of years in the hip pocket of George Smith. My father made his rounds on the sports circuit as sports editor of The Anniston Star, starting as a copy boy in the mid-'50s. Always running, always busy, always fun. The company he kept had names like Bear, Shug, Joe Willie, Splendid Splinter, Hee Haw, Snake and others. They were all celebrities in some way, local or national, but just folks he got to talk to while earning the family keep.

Many times this little blond-haired boy got to tag along. My father was never in the same place very long. Dad's office was the hood of a car, a shade tree, a sweaty dressing room or the quietest table he could find at the nearest pub or grease joint.

Whether sitting, standing, riding or trying to get to the center of a Tootsie Pop, I would listen. The cigarette smoke and words swirled around, seeming to blend together in the air above us and fall perfectly on the pages of the reporter's notebook he always pulled out of his coat or back pocket.

Mom, "the Blonde," kept the home fires burning and the skillet hot. While I would embellish our latest adventure over the sizzle of salmon patties, Dad would retreat to his closet office and start to transcribe his stories from the scribbled notes only he could decipher. The tap tap tapping, ding and zzziiiip! would come racing out of the old Underwood typewriter, well ahead of the coffee and cigarettes, bouncing off every floor, wall and ceiling in the house. The story had begun.

This was the life for my dad for over 20 years. But he was just warming up. His stories were about sports, but mostly about the people who played in what he called "America's Toy Shop." From Augusta to Seattle and New York to Miami, it was the people inside the Toy Shop that fascinated him.

When H. Brandt Ayers, boss and publisher, talked to Dad about becoming The Star's general columnist in 1979, it was, as Dad would say later, a "no-brainer." No longer having to keep scores and stats at hand, or drive from Anniston to Tuscaloosa to Auburn and back in one day, Dad could now write the way he loved most. Just telling stories about the folks we all know.

Dad is a voracious reader, an observer of life, and sees the little things in daily living that most people busily walk past. His writing is the result of two traits that are rarely in the same person: living life fast and out loud, while at the same time having a contemplative, reflective awareness of what is going on around him.

Between these covers, you will join thousands of loyal readers who have picked up the paper for almost six decades just to see what George Smith had to say. You will understand why you would usually bump into somebody who asked, "Did you read George Smith's column today?" They are stories written in a style you can't learn, about people you wish you knew, usually from a perspective you haven't thought of.

Now if you will excuse me, someone told me I need to read George Smith's column today. Something about how I may not be in the will this week.

Barry Smith
"Son and Heir"

FAMILY

AN ESSAY ON THE TIES THAT BIND

MARCH 15, 2015

I am sitting on a stool in a closet in a house out on the edge of town.

The house belongs to the Blonde, but she's allowed me to hang out here for a number of years. I'm thankful for that, but this is a time for ...

Contemplating ...

What I'm doing in my time of contemplation is studying my tie rack; you know, those things that you tie around your neck and pull the knot until you can't breathe.

I'm a bit *tied*, too, because on my tie rack hang 31 ties ... *31 ties.*

There are solids, there are stripes, there are flowers, and a few that look like where a drunk lost the cause of his hangover. One other thing is, I didn't buy a single one of those ties.

Some were Christmas presents and some were birthday presents. I think a couple were Groundhog Day presents. I'm sure I got at least one for Valentine's Day, another for Labor Day. The beat goes on (left out Father's Day), and if I could catalogue all those dates I could throw away my Liberty National calendar.

Ties That Bind

One thing, in contemplating, a line from an old Eddy Arnold song keeps running through my mind:

"Jim, I wore a tie to town today,

"The first one I ever wore ..."

That comes to mind in looking at a photo of the very first tie I ever owned. It is wrapped around the neck of a small boy. He's really a good-looking kid, maybe 4 years old, but you can tell by the look on his face that he does not like the tie. Nor is he very fond of the dark suit and white shirt he is wearing.

Since we didn't get to town very much back then, I doubt I ever wore that tie to town. Probably for Easter, but not to town. But oh lordy, have I ever worn ties down through the years since. I have worn them to weddings, to funerals, to work, and to church on Sunday.

Now, I am down to wearing ties only when I am a pallbearer at a friend's funeral or to a friend's wedding. 'Course at my age, I don't have all that many friends getting married. I am thankful for that.

I am also thankful that I am not a preacher or an insurance agent, a banker or a car salesman or a basketball coach. All of those vocations come with ties around their necks.

Did I really *tie* in basketball coaches with ties?

Sure did. And for a good reason.

After Auburn's win over Texas A&M in the SEC tournament Thursday, one of those TV types (wearing a tie) stuck a mic in Coach Bruce Pearl's face with, "How many suits did you bring on this trip?"

The answer was four.

Each suit, of course, had to have a tie of its own. Which means a lot of heavy packing for the trip to Nashville.

But back to a closet in a house out on the edge of town and more *contemplating*.

Just over the hill and down the road is a new Center of Hope building bigger than Bryant-Denny Stadium. There

3

is also a huge Center of Hope in Oxford, another in East Gadsden.

It's a good bet there's room for a few of my ties there, like 29 or so. That would leave me all I need, one tie for casket duty and one for weddings.

Did you mention going to church?

OK, one of the main attractions at Blue Mountain Baptist is we're casual in our dress code. And I do mean casual. On a recent Sunday morning, there were just *TWO* ties in the house. The preacher and one deacon were the only ones overdressed.

It's amazing what a loose collar can do for you on Sunday morning inside a 30-minute sermon.

There's more I could put in this little essay, but I've got to get 29 ties out of the closet in a house out on the edge of town to the Center of Hope before a certain blonde gets home.

Wish me luck ...

WHAT A WONDERFUL WORLD

AUGUST 14, 1991

The small stream really doesn't look like much. It meanders along, aimlessly, idly, pausing here and there to collect itself in small, quiet pools in shady nooks and crannies before succumbing to gravity's downhill pull and moving on.

But even in departing the pools, it is a mere trickle, hardly more than a kitchen faucet in need of a plumber's wrench.

The trickling over the water-smoothed stones and drifting twigs that form miniature dams is almost as quiet as the pools themselves. You have to listen closely to hear.

Seemingly, the small stream is in no particular hurry to get wherever it is it's going.

Unseen by the heavy traffic pounding past on McClellan Boulevard, the moving water is also mostly ignored by those who use the walking trail at Lagarde Park to lose unwanted fat while rebuilding aging lungs.

It is not ignored by small boys.

...

For small boys — perhaps small girls, too — the tiny stream captivates and delights. The winding ditch it calls home is a place of great exploration, home of skittering water beetles, flittering butterflies, hovering dragonflies and rocks that explode when correctly hurled against other rocks.

And who knows what deadly creatures — man-eating snakes, for sure — lurk beneath the overhanging banks in those bends where the clear, graveled bottom of the shallows blend into the shaded blackness of deeper depths?

Such places, in case you've forgotten, are proving grounds, a place in the growing road as timid boyhood takes early tests for future manhood.

It is good that adult walkers, huffing uphill near the tiny stream, go their own way. The small boys in the stream have no need for, nor do they want, an adult's presence.

...

But there is a grandfather who thanks three small boys for letting him, for a too-brief afternoon, relive just a little of his own boyhood, albeit from a nonintrusive if supervisory distance.

It came just this past week in the grandfather's desperate attempt to find something, anything, just one thing, that would provide quiet respite from a grandchild-sitting assignment.

The grandfather sat on the bank, back against a tree. He did little if any supervising. Mostly he watched, remained silent ... and wished he could, for a time, be 5 years old again ... or 6 or 9.

There was no rushing to the rescue when the smallest, early on, used a slippery, red clay bank as an excuse to get a sliding start into one of the small pools.

Nor was there a reprimand when another, with great delight, sent a rather large rock splashing between his two brothers, setting off a flurry of splashing rocks and muddy showers for all.

Neither was there any alarm when the three, led by the smallest, discovered all the wonderful forms red clay can take when wet and hand-molded by young imagination.

...

After all, figured the grandfather, there's nothing about red, wet clay, even from toe-tip to head-tip, that a good hosing-down won't cure.

If memories are the soft cushion of life (as pro golfer Gary Player once said), the grandfather was sitting in a very comfortable place.

He, too, had once slid down muddy banks in small streams, had splashed others with hurled stones and had painted himself into a real Indian warrior with red, wet clay.

He had also, with great and chilling trepidation, dared to explore beneath overhanging banks for the sorts of dangers that, if escaped or conquered, turn a three-foot boy into a six-foot man, especially in the telling.

What a wonderful world that had been.

What a wonderful world this one afternoon had been, too.

Thanks, guys.

We're gonna do it again.

For one thing, it's considerably cheaper than that new plaything at Burger King.

For another, it's fun.

REMEMBER, MOM, WHEN I WAS A KID?

MAY 12, 2002

"But the child's mother said, 'As surely as the Lord lives and as you live, I will not leave you.' So he got up and followed her." — **2 Kings 4:30**

Flora Cobb Smith died sometime during the afternoon of June 3, 1995.

At the time of her death, she was quilting, sitting near a window where the light was good. The needle was still in the quilt, a thimble on the middle finger of her right hand.

We found her the next morning, a Sunday; buried her on a Tuesday, June 6 ... the birthdate of a daughter who had died in a car accident at age 21.

Flora Cobb Smith was my mother, and she has never left me.

And this morning, Mother's Day, 2002, she will be sitting with me in the fifth pew from the back, at Blue Mountain Baptist Church.

The Rev. Bob Ford, a good and decent man, will bring the message, and a good bet is it will be about the good and decent women who were, are, or will be, mothers.

I will listen, but perhaps not with full attention, not while my mother is with me.

We'll not speak, of course, but memories run on silent are just as warming as if spoken.

Remember, Mom, when I was just a kid and "ran away from home?"

You knew where I was all the time, in the woods ... within sight of the house.

Mom, I sure remember when it got dark and I wanted to come home and you stood in the edge of the yard with a dogwood brush broom and wouldn't let me near the house for the longest of time.

I never ran away again, did I, Mom?

And remember, Mom, after Dad died and we went to lunch every Thursday?

My, how you loved cheeseburgers and fries, Mom. I'd just about wash behind my ears, Mom, if I could take you out and buy you just one more cheeseburger.

And I remember, Mom, two things you always said ... every Thursday.

You'd look at the waitresses and say, "I always wanted to work in a café when I was a girl, but my daddy wouldn't let me. After I got married, your daddy wouldn't let me, either."

Then there was all that traffic on Quintard.

You'd shake your head and say, "I don't know where all these people come from. It's a good thing I never learned to drive or I'd be out here burning up the roads myself."

Mom, I ran your picture in the paper this morning. I know you've never had your picture in the paper before, but I wanted everybody to see how pretty you were back then.

I'll always be proud you were my mom, and I'm really glad you wore that pretty blue dress to church this morning.

And I will talk to you next week ...

I DON'T LIKE CHANGE

AUGUST 11, 1993

I'm the sort of person who doesn't like change.

I still believe my first car, a '49 Ford coupe with overdrive, was the best I've ever owned. I also see nothing wrong with wearing bell-bottom pants, white socks, and blue denim shirts.

In my world, Roy Acuff is still king of country music – always has been, always will be – and Garth Brooks is an aberration with the talent of a cactus plant.

Best I can figure, the last "modern" convenience I approved of was filter-tip cigarettes.

Non-filtered Chesterfields had a tendency to stick, leaving me with a bloody lower lip.

I'm the sort of person who doesn't give up a pair of shoes until the cobbler offers a new pair just to keep from patching the old ones ... again.

Material possessions, with me, become old friends, and to give up something I've become comfortable with is an emotionally draining experience.

I STILL remember the afternoon I came home from work to find my favorite chair, a battered old platform rocker, sitting out on the patio. It wasn't the first time a certain lady had tossed the old rocker out. It was the first time she had done so in the middle of a typhoon.

"I'd like to see you haul it back in this time," is basically what she said. What I said is unprintable and came darn near being evidence in a divorce.

With all that said, I'm pretty sure I can come up with enough to fill out today's column on what I really wanted to say, which is:

I said goodbye to an old friend recently.

The date was July 31 – a date of no large significance other than it was my birthday. But among the presents my beloved family showered me with was a new wallet (that's city talk for billfold).

I HAVE never been bashful about accepting gifts. Receiving is something of which I wholeheartedly approve, and if there is any doubt as to what I'd like for my birthday – for Christmas, for Father's Day, for Groundhog Day, for whatever – I'm willing to compile a list.

A new wallet (city talk for billfold) was not on my July 31, 1993, request sheet. The old one had been riding my hip for the past 22 years or so and had come to me from a 9-year-old kid who calls Florence, Italy, home. The "kid" is now 32.

I came to treasure that wallet (city talk for billfold) made of eelskin enough so that the pain of losing its predecessor finally eased and, in those 22 years, we became, as mentioned, very close friends.

Women may be sentimental about diamond rings and old love letters, but for a man, a wallet ranks right there with his watch and chain or best bird dog.

There is a dependency that goes beyond its mere purpose as a place for whatever money you might carry, including that little stash in the secret pocket you think your wife knows nothing about.

IN MY CASE, for 22 years, the eelskin wallet had also been home to pictures of my kids and then my grandkids, bank deposit slips, credit cards (balance due, of course), paycheck stubs, scraps of paper on which I had written important phone numbers (and then forgot to whom the numbers belonged), stamps, Social Security card, Blue Cross card, automobile insurance card, and et cetera and et cetera.

And while I really didn't want a new wallet (city talk for billfold), nothing lasts forever, not even eelskin ... even on an eel, I'm told.

To say my old friend (sentimental slop for billfold) was in ill repair is a major understatement. If there were coroners for wallets (city talk for billfolds), mine would have been pronounced dead a long time ago.

Even the "kid," in town for a visit, agreed with my family that it was time for a change, but that was of little comfort.

And I'll let you in on a little secret here: Had it not been a birthday gift I would have told 'em (the family) where to stick the new wallet. Why didn't I?

Hey, Labor Day is just around the corner and I have my list ready ...

YOU'LL NEVER HAVE ANOTHER MOTHER ...

MAY 10, 2015

"Have you called your momma today? I sure wish I could call mine." — **Paul "Bear" Bryant**

Memories sometimes fade with age and maybe your remembrance is not exactly the way the memory was born.

Doesn't matter, really, so long as ...

"The best place to cry is in your mother's arms." — Jodi Picoult

I have one memory that holds me close in memories of Flora Cobb Smith and the refuge I found in her arms.

I am 5 and playing with my sister. In a fit of anger, she pushes me from behind, breaking my arm across a big rock. Broken in two places, I can close my eyes and still see the "U" shape of the break.

The family doctor, a kindly man who loved to chew tobacco and drink whiskey, sets my arm.

Three weeks later, the kindly old doctor removes the splints (no casts back then), announces he has set my arm crooked. He corrects the problem by popping my arm across his knee and resetting the two breaks.

Yes, I did cry in my mother's arms that day.

"I realized when you look at your mother, you're looking at the purest love you will ever know." — Mitch Albom

In that I read a memory of my mother's purest love.

In my teenage years, it is normal for me to come home near midnight on Friday and Saturday.

The second I open the door, Mom comes out of her bedroom with "Are you hungry?" With no other words, she goes into the kitchen and fries cornbread. Fried cornbread in cold buttermilk is as good as it gets.

I'd love to have my Mom's fried cornbread in a glass of cold buttermilk just one more time.

"Behind all your stories is always your mother's stories because that's when yours begins." — Mitch Albom

I am in my fifth year and we are living in a two-room shack at the foot of a mountain. There is no water, no lights, and the roads are dirt.

In a fit over something or another, I tell Mom, "I'm running away."

She said, "Go."

It is a fun afternoon up in the mountains until the shadows began to lengthen. There are strange sounds in the mountains that scare a 5-year-old boy. I head home, can still see the coal oil light spilling out the kitchen door.

But when I step into the yard, my gentle little mother comes from nowhere, swinging a dogwood brush broom with:

"You're not coming in this yard or this house ever again. You ran away, now stay gone."

After about two years she gathers me in her arms and says:

"Come on in, I love you."

That is her story, just one of many I have of her. I never ran away again, but it took my adult years to realize I had again seen the purest of love.

"There is something about losing your mother that is permanent and inexpressible — A wound that will never quite heal." — Susan Wise

It is the "wound that will never quite heal" that brings memories of my mother in the quiet times, often at night as I drift into sleep.

In my memories, there is one I treasure that brings a smile.

Still in my fifth year, we have moved into an old, beat-up house near Chosea Springs. My dad is trying to teach Mom to drive.

In one trip around the house in an old Model A, Mom takes off a corner of the house. Didn't hurt the car, but Dad never again tried to teach her to drive, nor did I.

"Always love your mother because you'll never get another." — Unknown

This morning, I wish I could hand her a single red rose, take her to hear her baby son preach, sit across from her at the table and say "I love you, Mom."

Flora Cobb Smith is no longer with me, but her memories are. I can't call my mom, but I hope you can call yours.

And give her a single red rose.

IN THESE MEMORIES OF MY FATHER

FATHER'S DAY, JUNE 17, 2012

It is in the gloaming somewhere in Louisiana, autumn of 1940, and the father of three, including a brand new baby girl, is at the wheel of a dark green '39 Ford.

In a time of no interstates or McDonald's, the father pulls off the road and down a slight incline into a clearing on the banks of a quiet-running creek.

The family piles out, Mom spreads a red-checked tablecloth on the hood of the '39 Ford. I head for the creek.

Shortly, there is a call from the father: "Let's eat."

On the hood of the '39 Ford are open cans of sardines packed in mustard, a box of soda crackers and several bottles of warm Coke.

To this day, it's the best meal I have ever put in my mouth.

...

It is a cold, bitter day in early March. My dad and I are putting in the floor system on a bedroom addition at my house. I look at my father, look at his skinned hands, know the carpentry profession that had fed his family of seven had been a long, hard life.

I wondered why, despite other jobs he'd held, he always came back to the hammer and the saw. I asked if he liked what he did.

"I sure do, son. When I was a boy and we came in from the fields, I'd get Dad's hammer and saw out and build something. That was fun for me."

Somehow, after that, I felt a lot better about my dad's life.

...

My dad was not exactly the silent type, but when he had a message for his oldest son, it was brief and to the point. My rules for living under his hand were just two:

"Boy, if I catch you lying or stealing, I'll kill you."

Best I remember, that came somewhere in my pre-teen years. And while I knew he wouldn't really kill me, I knew he'd make me wish I were dead. The discipline of my formative years was hard ... and expected.

...

To say my dad used colorful language is an understatement, to say he liked the bottle on weekends is a fair statement. But not once in my entire life did my dad ever raise his voice or touch one of us when he was "on a toot."

...

It is a Sunday morning and Dad and his brother, my Uncle Tony, had fished the previous day away. Liberal doses of white whiskey had been consumed.

Out in the yard, I walk past Dad's '36 Ford panel truck and notice that the choke (on the dash) has been pulled out and bent down at a 90-degree angle.

Dad's answer?

"Aw, it was your Uncle Tony. He was driving too fast so I just pulled the choke out and bent it. That stopped him."

Later in the day, I mentioned the bent choke to Uncle Tony.

"Your daddy was driving too fast and I couldn't get him to slow down so I jerked the choke out. That stopped him."

To this day, I have no idea who was driving and who was doing the "choking." It's a good bet neither of them remembered, either.

...

My dad was not one to tarry at anything, even in his going away.

On a Sunday morning, he suffered the last of several strokes. This one was major.

On a Monday afternoon, May 8, 1990, I am standing by his bed in intensive care at RMC. He has not spoken or opened his eyes since the stroke.

I am holding his hand. I say, "Dad, I love you. If you can hear me, squeeze my hand."

He squeezed my hand ... twice. A few minutes later, he was gone.

He was five days shy of his 80th birthday. He had always said he wanted to live to be 80. In the obituary, I listed his age as 80.

It was the last thing I could do for him ... except to hold close the memories of the parts of him I know are in me.

BELIEVING GRANDPAPPY'S TALES

NOVEMBER 14, 2010

Up on the housetop,
Reindeer pause ...
... and out jumps good old "Ho-Ho-Ho!"

H ey, watch your mouth, friend.
Don't tell me there's no Santa Claus.
For one thing, anybody that can land a sleigh
on top of a steep roof has to be not only real, but also really
special.

Fact is, I used to stand in my grandfather's front yard a
day or so before Christmas and look up at his steep roof and
wonder at the wonder of it all. In my mind's eye, I could see
and hear the rush of Dasher and Dancer and their team-
mates rushing down from Bain's Gap toward Pleasant Ridge.

OK, so I never did really see Dasher and Dancer actually land — I was always asleep when they came — but I do
recall my grandfather once replacing shingles near the front
room chimney just after Christmas.

He told me there were holes in the shingles where Dasher
and Dancer had landed a bit hard. He said they'd probably
gotten tired coming all the way from the North Pole and had
been "a little careless on their approach."

If you can't believe your grandpappy's tales ...
So what got a fully-growed man into this ... this morning?
Blame it on the newspaper.

Got it out of the box the other day and the first thing that fell out was a "Toyland Catalog 2010" from my favorite general store, Walmart. The turkey hasn't even been thawed, and suddenly "'Tis the season."

Thumbing through 52 pages of toys was remindful of Christmas strolls through Woolworth's and Kress's and Silver's (or do you remember?) in years past.

But one thing bothered me.

There was not a single picture of Santa to be found in the 52 pages of toys. There was this little elf here and there, but no St. Nick. I wondered if political correctness had caught up with "The Night Before."

Surely not ... at least it hasn't at Fred's, another one of my favorite places to walk around and try to NOT buy things NOT on the list handed me by the blonde.

For that, I place in evidence the Fred's insert that came with my Sunday paper a week ago.

At the bottom of the first page was old "Ho-Ho-Ho" himself. He was holding a big sign touting lower prices "for the season." There was even a "28-inch LED Santa Claus Yard Ornament" that could be yours for $20.

And while I have seen Santa imposters down at Quintard Mall and ringing bells on Noble Street, it is true I've actually never seen the old man himself.

But I've been in his presence.

At least twice in my early years, in the dark of an old farmhouse in Choccolocco Valley, I heard him out in the front room.

I knew it was him because there was an old man's shuffle to the steps and also a good bit of whispering. It was evident he'd brought along an elf or two for assistance.

It sent a chill through my soul and, frankly, I was too scared to get up and take a look.

But I'm going to own up to one thing — and I hope he doesn't hold this against me this Christmas — but I haven't always been happy with the old gentleman.

It was 1942 and I was fighting a courageous war against hordes of German and Japanese soldiers that had invaded my valley.

In need of advanced weaponry, I'd sent word to Santa that I would like a brace (two) of six-shooters. Instead, I got a two-shot pirate's pistol. I'm still amazed that I won World War II with such a primitive weapon.

In retrospect, Santa knew exactly what he was doing ... and that is also proof he is real.

Which means I gotta get started on "making my list and checking it twice."

'FREE:' HE WAS THE BEST FRIEND I EVER HAD

FEBRUARY 21, 2010

From my memories, I can still see him ...
  – Kneeling beside a clear mountain spring and, with one hand, scooping water to his mouth. Kneeling beside him, I do the same.
  – Bending slightly at the knees as he heads up the mountain, a .22 rifle riding the back of his neck, one arm dropped over the barrel, the other over the stock. Just behind him, I am doing the same.
  – Head bent, a flat-top guitar cradled on his right knee, he is picking *The Wildwood Flower*. He then lays the guitar across his lap and, using his pocket knife as a slide bar, turns the flat-top into a Dobro. I sit just in front of him and listen to the lilting runs of his fingers and wish I could do the same.
  – With his dad's single-shot .22 pressed against his cheek, he levels the barrel at a kitchen match stuck in a post exactly 20 paces away and pulls the trigger. With the flat pop of the bullet, the match, exactly 20 paces away, ignites, but never moves. He replaces the match, I take the rifle and, for one fleeting second I am just as good. He has taught me the secret. Put a bullet within two inches of the match head and friction does the rest.

– In a maroon 1940 Ford coupe, he is teaching my grandmother to drive. They speed through the yard, miss six pine trees and go over a 20-foot bluff in front of the house. I find him sitting with his back to a pine tree. I can see his teeth through a gaping gash in his right cheek. I kneel and I cry and, for one of the very few times in my life, I don't want to be him.

– Home on leave from the Marine Corps before heading to the South Pacific and horrors he refuses to discuss, ever. I read the newspapers of battles on Guadalcanal and Iwo Jima and I wish I were with him.

– After the war is over and he comes home, he is leaving his chair and running toward a strange car pulling into the backyard. A stranger gets out and the two hug, slap each other's backs ... and cry. It is the first time I have ever seen grown men cry. The stranger is a war buddy and he was "over there" with him.

– Riding "shotgun" with me as I drive to Tuscaloosa and Auburn and Birmingham, me to write football for this newspaper, he as my buddy along the way.

– Standing in the middle of a logging road looking up into a sky framed by tall trees. He is "tracking" the wild bee to its "honey tree." I am with him and one summer we cut and harvest the wild honey from three trees.

– Standing by the huge tire of a John Deere tractor, cutting a plug from a chunk of Day's Work chewing tobacco. He hands the plug up to me, says it will get me through 'til noon at least. I become very sick and the furrows I am plowing look like a snake track in the sand. I'm not sure I like him any longer.

– Sitting by a lantern deep in the mountains waiting for his big Redbone hound to send up the steady chant that says he has treed a possum. He has a pint jar of white whiskey and offers me a pull. He laughs with delight when I choke and spit and utter a few cuss words I suspect I'd heard from him.

– His forever smile getting wider and his blue eyes lighting with delight as I walk in. He gets up and wraps me in a big hug and I finally understand that long-ago afternoon in my grandfather's backyard when he and a stranger hugged and cried.

– Laying in a hospital bed, looking up at me in recognition even though he is very, very ill. I see the curtain come down in his eyes and feel his grip falter. He is going away, this time forever, and I know there is nothing I or anyone else can do. A God he has great faith in is by the bed, too, has come for his spirit ... and his soul.

– I hear the preacher at his funeral saying:

"He was a man who loved deeply and hated very little ..."

He was my uncle ... Freeman Smith, the best friend I ever had on this earth ... or ever will.

OUR FAMILY GOT A MIRACLE THIS TIME

OCTOBER 8, 2000

There was another wreck at the intersection of U.S. 431 and Lenlock Lane this past week.

Thursday morning, a heavily loaded dump truck, headed north on U.S. 431, plowed into the side of a GMC Yukon.

In the Yukon were my son, two of my grandsons and two other young people.

Folks, miracles do happen.

My youngest grandson, Cody Smith, was admitted to Regional Medical Center, but his injuries are not life-threatening. Blake Brodeur, Cody's buddy, possibly has a broken arm, but was dismissed following treatment.

There were no fatalities.

Other families have not been so blessed.

Back in December, just two days before Christmas, two young men lost their lives at the same intersection.

They were Ashley Doyle, age 21, and Josh Gaither, age 22. Another young man, David Jolly of Gadsden, age 20, was charged with driving under the influence. That was later upgraded to two counts of murder.

In just one accident, two young lives ended, a third will in all probability do jail time. He certainly will live his life regretting the split second that ushered two other lives into eternity.

At the time, I was asked — and I considered — writing a column about that December incident. While I did not know the two young men who were killed, they were friends of my oldest grandson, both well known and well respected in the community.

For whatever reason, I did not write about that accident or about those young men.

But the truth is, even had I done so, in no way would it have prevented what happened to my son, my two grand-sons and two other young people Thursday morning.

Answers for the problems at this particular intersection seem hard to come by.

It is a problem intersection, always has been. And that, in itself, is a puzzle.

Sight lines from all directions are as good as you could want. Headed north or south on 431, the traffic lights at the intersection are visible for at least a mile. Coming into the highway from Lenlock Lane, the light is visible for at least a quarter of a mile.

The problem?

One, without a doubt, is the speed limit. It is 65 mph ... and the traffic is consistently heavy.

The other is human failings ... a rush to get there before then, a contempt for law, a complete disregard of human life, of the damage we can do to others.

And such seems of no particular interest to anyone ... until it affects us, as in we or me or whomever.

Standing at the foot of Cody's bed Thursday afternoon, looking at the tubes connecting body to machines and watching, with bated breath of my own, the near indiscernible rise and fall of his chest with each shallow breath, will haunt me the rest of my life.

It will be the same for his mom, his dad, his brothers, his other grandparents, all of whom were in the room.

Sadly, both sets of Cody's grandparents are no strangers to the death of a child.

My wife and I lost a son at age 20. Helen and J.C. Robinson, Cody's maternal grandparents, lost a daughter at age 17 in a terrible accident. Another daughter, age 19, struggled for life several days before winning.

Every time a young life is lost, incredible and never-ending heartache is the legacy. Other families besides ours know that. Sadly, others will come to know it, too.

This time, dear God, we were spared.

And this morning, whether headed to church, to Grandma's house, or for a biscuit out on the highway, please, please be careful ... of others as well as yourself.

Remember just one thing: We are all, every single one of us, just one heartbeat away from eternity.

GEORGE SMITH

THE BLONDE

A STORY OF LOVE AND COURTSHIP

FEBRUARY 13, 2011

I'll be yours, if you'll be mine;
Everything will be so fine,
If you will be my valentine ...

I have no idea who wrote that, but I heard it in first grade when the teacher drew a heart on the blackboard along with the lyrics. She then led us in song.

It didn't help me all that much, certainly not with this cute little girl with bobbed hair who had smiled at me from across the room. She had no idea what that smile did to my six-year-old heart ...

When I tried to "solo" her with the song during recess, she ran howling into the room and I hid under the schoolhouse. I can still hear the hoots of derision.

Now, let me fast-forward to my late teens and a very beautiful blonde for whom I had developed a magnificent obsession and (at the time) unrequited love.

Somewhere in there, I ran across this in a book ...

"For this was on seynt Volantynys day,
"Whan euery bryd comyth there to chese his make."

(That's from Chaucer's "Parlement of Foules," written in 1382, and the very first recorded association of Valentine's Day with romantic love.)
Translated, you get:
"For this was Saint Valentine's Day, when every bird cometh there to choose his mate."
I clipped it from the book and spent time out on the back porch in song, getting myself ready for a rare Saturday-night date with my unrequited love.

At the drive-in movie, I put my arm around her car seat, hummed a few bars and let go with:
"For this was Saint Valentine's Day, when every bird cometh ..."
Shades of yesteryear ...
Opening the door on her side, she managed (around giggles) to say, "I gotta go to the restroom." I can still see her shoulders shaking as she headed toward the concession stand.

Me?

I thought about just leaving her there. But then it occurred to me she had two brothers (one bigger than me) and one daddy (also bigger than me). We drove home in silence.

But I am persistent if nothing else.

Poetry in song, especially delivered by my less-than-melodious pipes, just didn't work, not on this very beautiful blonde with whom I had developed a magnificent obsession and (at the time) unrequited love.

I forgot about becoming the next Frank Sinatra (OK, out our way it was Hank Williams ... we didn't know any Sinatras). I got serious with such stuff as telling her what she wanted to hear, which is the essence of any successful courtship. I also pitched in some chocolate candy (when I could afford it) and roses (got those from my grandmother's rose bushes) along the way.

Also along the way, on every date I'd greet her with "Will you marry me?" I also said good night with "Will you marry me?"

I knew I was making progress because she was no longer laughing at me, even holding my hand every other Saturday night or so.

Then came the "yes," which she didn't really say.

On a Saturday night, driving into a sweeping curve in front of Hebron Baptist Church, I hear ...

"You know, I think I really would like an engagement ring."

I hit both ditches and a picnic table in the churchyard before I got that old '49 Ford straightened out.

I was at Couch's Jewelers Monday morning at 10 a.m., promising to pay $5 a month on a diamond for the rest of my natural life. She's still got the diamond, and I've still got her.

Happy Valentine's Day, sweetheart ... and ...

"I'll be yours, if you'll be mine."

Hey, I have to get out of here and go buy some candles and candy ...

OK, FOLKS, JUST 'LISTEN' TO ME

AUGUST 11, 2013

"My wife said I never listen. At least I think that's what she said."

That little jewel is posted in my barn just to the right of a 46-inch, hi-def TV. The barn is where I spend a lot of time in a recliner watching Colin Cowherd, college football, World War II, the Discovery Channel and the Atlanta Braves.

I also spend some time with Merle and Willie and books by W.E.B. Griffin.

The blonde put it there on a day I was having breakfast with some buddies at the Citgo station just outside Woodland. And truth is, I don't have the guts to take it down, not even when she's hanging out at Dillard's.

But the main reason I mention "My wife said I never listen. At least I think that's what she said" are all the notices I get from a local hearing-aid business offering me all sorts of deals in order for me to hear my wife a bit better.

At least, I think that's the reason. I honestly believe that somewhere down the line, when I really wasn't listening, the blonde called the hearing aid people and gave them my name and address.

The reason I believe that is two-fold:

1. She really does claim (quite frequently) that I don't listen.

2. All the letters claiming to improve my hearing are addressed to me, NEVER to my wife.

One place I hear that I don't listen is when we're in the kitchen. She's at the counter putting together yet another out-of-sight dish, I'm sitting at the table. She is talking, I am grunting. She turns, I am reading the latest edition of Time magazine ...

"George Smith, you NEVER listen to me!"

When your beloved addresses you by first and last name, you've got a problem, a big one.

But I digress a wee bit.

So, back to the hearing aid company and its concern for the condition of my hearing. Over the last few months, I've called and asked that my name be removed from their mailing list. I tell them that I can hear a pin drop across the street, that I am NOT hard of hearing, regardless of what the blonde claims.

But the mail keeps coming, which, if nothing else, helps a United States Postal Service that is not just going broke, but is already bankrupt. And has been for quite a while.

And while I really do listen (when it suits me, but don't let the blonde know I said that ... PLEASE), the local hearing aid folks need to know that I can read, if not hear. But when I see their name on the letter, I DON'T read. On my way back to the house from the mailbox I detour by the garbage can.

The sound of the garbage can lid falling on a hearing aid brochure is pleasing to the ear. It is also proof that I really can hear.

But I should be thankful the hearing aid folks are taking a pass on using my email box to hustle my business.

I use an email different from the one you see in the newspaper. It's the one advertisers from coast to coast have in their computers. This week, in just three days, that mailbox had a whopping 87 mailings.

Which is another reason the Postal Service is headed for extinction. There was a time, before the Internet, that you didn't count your junk mail, you weighed it. Over the last three days, I've gotten 87 offers in my email, had exactly six junk mails via the mailman.

Anyway, I gotta go.

I need a little dose of Tennessee Ernie Ford's hymnal before heading for church, which proves I really do listen ... when it suits me.

But I've said that already, haven't I?

SMOKING IS ALL THE WAY TO TOENAILS

NOVEMBER 20, 2003

"Quitting smoking is easy. I've done it a thousand times."
– Mark Twain

Best I remember, I've quit smoking four times.

The first time lasted about six months, my relapse coming on a hot, summer day in the middle of Fink's Lake in Saks. The fish were on vacation and my friend had a pack of Camels in his tackle box.

One wouldn't hurt, right?

Wrong.

My next two relapses are sort of blurry. On one occasion the blonde caught me sneaking a puff behind the house. Disgusted, she slept on the couch a couple of nights before finally giving up on my lousy character and returning to the wedded bed.

The fourth relapse?

Hasn't happened yet ... and come 4:30 a.m. on Jan. 6, 2004, it will be four years since I've had one single, solitary puff. That's four wonderful years.

The reason I'm jumping the gun on the anniversary is today is Great American Smokeout Day. What you do in observance of Great American Smokeout Day is if you're a smoker you go 24 hours without a cigarette.

Sounds easy, but it isn't ... not from my experience.

I remember one Great American Smokeout Day that I decided to observe.

At 7 a.m. on the dot, I pulled my "smokes" from my shirt pocket and locked them in my desk. I then walked up the hall to the bathroom and flushed the key to my desk down the toilet.

At 7:01 a.m. the next morning, I jimmied the desk lock and, at 7:02:39, pulled a long draw of smoke all the way to my toenails.

That may sound a bit far-fetched, but it's close enough to pass a polygraph. I tell it to tell you that while I have white fingernails again, I still remember the insidious hold tobacco can have on your very soul.

And I will not tell you that I have forgotten just how wonderful those things taste. I won't insult your intelligence with that.

But I can tell you that I have lost my craving. It was easy, too, but one I don't recommend.

In the fall of '99, a visit to the doctor came with the words, "You have a malignancy." My first thought, honestly, was: "Damn, I'm not gonna live to get to the house."

The cancer had nothing to do with smoking. Until surgery two months later took care of the cancer, I continued to puff away.

But at 4:30 a.m., Jan. 6, 2000, standing outside St. Vincent's Hospital with a knife an hour or so away, I remember flipping aside a cigarette with, "Well, it'll be a few days before I get another."

The days are now stretching near four years.

It can be done, folks. And today is as good a time to start as you're going to find.

But one other thing. Please don't consider this a sermon. It's merely a little slice of one ex-smoker's life.

It's your choice ... as always.

Oh, one other thing. Best I can figure, my abstinence has given the blonde an extra $8,760 or so to spend. Makes her happy ... and when she's happy, I'm happy.

A YARD OUT OF WINTER
IS REALLY UGLY

MAY 17, 2015

WHEN YOU start defining ugly, put a yard coming out of a hard winter at the top of the list. And we did have a hard winter which, if nothing else, gave those who do such things another excuse to push completion of the Eastern Parkway back again.

Which, in itself, is two things:

1. A cheap shot.
2. Nothing to do with today's sermon.

With that said, gimme an "Amen!" and let's move along.

At the moment, the Blonde is into her annual Yard Beautification Project and I'm trying very hard to stay out of the way and not be helpful.

At her side is Jerry Dobbins, who lives down the street and does a lot of Yard Beautification for a lot of people.

Word is Jerry is pretty good at turning Winter Yard Ugly into a garden just this side of Eden. Just watching the Blonde and Jerry stoop and bend and scrape and plant pains my back. Before the Yard Beautiful is finished, I'll eat a bottle of Tylenol without lifting a finger.

A couple of things here:

1. I've done a really good job of staying out of their way, happy in my role as a spectator.

2. Off the results of her past spring magic, I know it's just a matter of time before Southern Living calls about Yard Beautiful.

The Blonde even made a couple of trips of her own to Lowe's out on Alabama 21. The trips were for the trimmings out back that will, at least to the eye, turn our backyard into a Better Homes and Gardens photo shoot. OK, maybe her design isn't quite that far up the ladder, but on those quiet summer evenings, twilight visiting on the patio is about as good as it gets.

Sometimes, believe it or not, we even get through an evening without her coming up with one of those "tomorrow-you-need-to ..." deals.

I shouldn't have said that about "you need to."

She has just opened the door to my man cave with:

"You need to go to Lowe's, pick up some dirt and also here's a list of a few more plants I need.

"You also need to run by Walmart and pick up the cheapest Pampers they have. They help hold the water."

And no, I didn't point out the obvious, that the purpose of Pampers really is to hold water. I haven't lost my mind entirely.

Of course, I do as I'm told. Someone once said that for a happy marriage a man needs to keep his pocketbook open and his mouth shut.

Anyway, back from Lowe's and Walmart, I return to my cave, put Willie and Merle on the stereo and watch as Exterior Decorator cuts and tears and mixes what used to be perfectly good Pampers with dirt.

The neighbor from down the street watches and sort of shakes his head. But a bit of good news is we now have enough Pampers to take care of our two great-granddaughters right through potty-trained.

Somewhere in there it occurs to me that I will probably use a few of those Pampers myself when Jerry gets through ... not for the bottom, but for the tears that will flood the patio when Jerry hands me his bill.

Thing is, he's not through yet.

He and Exterior Decorator have agreed that the patio now needs a power wash.

His grin is getting wider by the moment.

Reading back over this essay on the perils of love and marriage, I need to say a couple of things.

In using Eden and Better Homes and Gardens and Southern Living, I may have been a bit immodest. Better Homes and Gardens will suffice.

I also know one of the best things I ever did for my physical and mental wellbeing was leaving my grandfather's farm in my 19th year.

Trouble is, in becoming a homeowner I traded the farm for a sump hole ...

A CHAPTER IN THE DEATH OF CIVILITY

SEPTEMBER 28, 2009

CHATTANOOGA, Tenn. — There is a parking lot ...
A Super 8 motel sign is outlined in a cloud-scuffed sky behind a block-long building sitting hard beside the hum of Interstate 75 as it turns south into Georgia.

A sign above one of a number of such shops in the complex reads "East Town Antiques."

Directly beneath is another sign ... "Entrance."

The antique malls pull travelers as well as locals off I-75.

Somewhere inside East Town, a blonde winds her way through the vendor booths. She moves at the speed of drying concrete and crawling molasses.

Outside, in the parking lot, a man is listening to Merle Haggard on the stereo and working his way through *The Salamander*, a novel by Morris West that was first published in 1975.

The man loves to read, and he buys a lot of books in a lot of East Towns. Two things about that: Used books are cheap. Secondly, if the man has not read the book, it is new to him.

The man is not the only life in the parking lot ...

He watches a man with receding gray hair and a woman with dark hair and a blue purse hanging from one hand walk across the parking lot. From a distance, she looks younger than him. Up close, she is aging, too, and has a tired look in her face. They do not speak.

The man in the truck wonders if they've ever really had much at all to say to each other.

Another couple, a young one in a small, dark blue SUV, parks. The woman, a blonde with stringy hair, removes a foldable baby carriage from the back of the SUV. She struggles to open the carriage. She struggles to move a baby from car seat to carriage. The husband stands idly by. He does not offer to help. They do not speak, one to the other, either.

After a while, an elderly man pushes an obscenely obese woman across the parking lot. He is painfully skinny and bent at the waist, arms extended full length as he labors in transport. There is no conversation.

Another young couple crosses the huge parking lot. The woman is pushing her baby in another one of those portable carriages. The man walks a good six steps in front of her and the baby. Neither do they talk.

After a while, the man in the truck replaces Merle with Willie and returns to *The Salamander*.

It is a novel of a conspiracy to return totalitarian government to Italy in the mid-1950s. It is a preachy book, a dark book, and full of not-very-nice people.

Willie eventually gives way to the news on the radio and there is a report that the House of Representatives has "admonished" Congressman Joe Wilson for yelling "You lie!" at the president during his speech last week on health care.

Somebody on the radio is wondering whatever happened to common civility in our political forums.

It occurs to the man in the truck that civility is dead in the great parking lots of America, as well.

He is saddened ... but not for the first time ... nor the last.

OUTLINED IN THE BLUE,
A RED ROSE

OCTOBER 16, 2011

'Tis the last rose of summer
Left blooming alone;
All her lovely companions
Are faded and gone ...
— **Thomas Moore**

My last rose of summer was something of a surprise. It was an hour or so past good daylight when I glanced over the privacy fence at the north end of the house. A tiny red bit of a gone summer's last breath, it was hanging just under the eaves of the house with a pale blue sky, sort of a Carolina blue, as a backdrop.

My last rose of summer was the only sign of life in the climbing vine of thorns that just yesterday — or so it seemed — had been draped in red. There were no other blooms, no other buds, no leaves from the ground all the way up to the last rose.

I stood there in the quiet of an empty morning, not yet busy with work-bound traffic for the longest time. For some reason, I felt as if I were looking at something very profound, but couldn't quite figure out what.

It crossed my mind maybe God was in the rose and He was trying to tell me something. But again, I wasn't sure as to what. Just an hour past good light, I was still, hopefully, sin-free for the day.

The rose was beautiful, no doubt about that. Sort of made me think of Valentine's Day, but that celebration of love was yet three cold winter months away.

Maybe it was the loneliness of the single rose that was so startling, maybe that was what held me to the spot at the fence ... and in the moment.

That loneliness deepened as I looked around. For good reason, too. In a corner of the privacy fence, just steps away, were three Knock Out Rose bushes gone dormant. Same for two Knock Outs out by the drive. Those, like the "climber" at the corner of the house, will be back in the spring. There will be lovely pink to support the red of the "climber."

After a while, I found a pair of pruning shears and clipped the rose from the vine, leaving a thorny stem of maybe 10 inches.

"Love thou the rose, yet leave it on its stem." — **Edward Bulwer-Lyton**

A tiny bud vase on the kitchen counter became home for the small rose. A few green leaves tucked around the rose were "just right."

From such small things ...

When the blonde turned out of the hallway into the kitchen for her first cup of coffee, there was, "What in the ..."

Talk about brownie points, not to mention two (not just one) hugs.

"Love and a red rose can't be hid." — **Thomas Holcroft**

So, for several days, it sat there ... bright red against the deep blue ceramic counter.

It made me feel good every time I reached for the coffeepot in the morning, comforted me as I made my way through the kitchen at night and down the hall to bed.

But the thing I liked most in the six or seven days it was there is the blonde not once moved it elsewhere. Seems she sort of liked it, too.

Friday late came a finish.

The last rose of summer didn't die, it simply shed its petals. And even at that, when I pulled the rose from the vase and dropped it in the trash, two tiny petals clung tightly to the stem.

"The rose that lives its little hour is prized beyond the sculptured flower." — **William C. Bryant**

Now ... before you get carried away with my knowledge of all things "rose," you should know Google helped me a bit. You know what I mean.

Next?

Well, you'll have to excuse me for a moment.

I've got to get the electric blanket out of the closet ...

FOR MOM, IT'S ALWAYS THE SON ...

MAY 14, 2006

For Mother's Day, son and heir Barry Smith takes over the column and writes himself out of his dad's will.

D ad calls her the blonde. He's afraid of her. I call her Mom, and I'm not afraid of her.

Is this the way of the world, or just of our clan?

That two men so alike can love the same woman, come running at the faintest sign of need or demand, and yet, for each of our equal actions, there is no equal reaction.

So, "Yea me!" the son, the heavier weight on the scales of affection.

Mother's Day 2006, 1906, or 6 BC, it doesn't matter. There is forever a special bond between mothers and their sons.

And I understand my subject well, for I am also the father of sons, three of them. At my house, that means I'm the featherweight.

I am not the king of my castle, and, thanks to my mom, I've long understood that the castle belongs to the prince.

These are not the rantings of a royal wannabe. I'm special. Ask my mom.

For more than a few days, my semi-blonde has been "in college," with THE boys. A medical need demanded her attention, leading to extended duties of medicine distribution, hygienic rooms, clean clothes, hot meals and lots of TLC.

Woe is me, right? Not so fast, my friend.

In the wife's absence, I "suffered" through two hot meals a day and leftovers that assured my survival through the night.

The neighbor's dog, Dixie, thought I'd moved in with Mom. The smells from the kitchen froze her to the back door, tail a'wagging.

After the usual two plates and a Diet Pepsi from my stash of 24 cans (thanks, Mom!), and a short nap in Dad's chair, I leave Mom's house a walking billboard for Ziploc bags, foil and Tupperware.

And with a leftover biscuit or two in my pocket to confirm Dixie's faith in my mom.

There is a downside to Mom's great love for her son: the pain in Dad's eyes as a midnight fridge raid walks out the door. He also knows next day's lunch is gone.

But it's a guilt trip I can live with. Besides, he can take care of himself. He's a grown man.

Any casual observation of life proves I live on a crowded pedestal. Have you ever seen a mom NOT defend her son? Adolf Hitler had a keen sense of invincibility. He always carried a picture of his mother. Connect the dots.

Attitudes are developed early. Mine began at an early age in the '50s. I'm sure Dad was full of pride, having fathered a son. I'm also sure he had no idea he had been replaced.

Future events clued him in. Small things, such as chocolate milk over white, pancakes and syrup instead of sausage and eggs ... *Star Trek* instead of *Gunsmoke* on the TV.

Full understanding of his standing came with Mom's dreaded, "I'm telling your dad." In the midst of my punishment for high crimes and misdemeanors, she'd call a halt.

She'd also give Dad the cold shoulder for at least two days for mistreating "HER son."

For mothers, it's always about the son ... to stand behind, to push and encourage, to pet and comfort.

And we, the sons, can live with the forever surety that there is one place where sons are always special ... home.

So, from the prince to the queen:

Happy Mother's Day, Mom ... and I love you so ...

WINTER ROSES?
MAYBE ON A MAGAZINE COVER

NOVEMBER 16, 2014

Faded love and winter roses ...

I 'm lucky.
    I don't know much about "faded love" except what I hear in some of those old sad country songs that I love, especially *Faded Love and Winter Roses.*

The late David Houston, who had one of the better voices ever in country music (or pop, too, for that matter) had a big hit on that one. There's another one called *Faded Love* that has been covered by just about everybody since the late Bob Wills and his Texas Playboys hit the top of the country charts with it in 1950.

(It occurs to me I now use "late" an awful lot in "stuff" I write.)

I married the only girl I ever loved. We've been together long enough to have one great-grandchild and another on the way. That takes care of the faded love business, 'cept maybe the times I walk past a certain line and get reminded that ... ain't going there!

Oh well, what you've just endured is a roundabout way to the winter roses.

Sadly, there is no such thing at the Smith Manor except on the cover of a few Home and Garden magazines beside the Blonde's chair.

Oh, we have roses for sure, several bushes of Knock Outs, some red, some pink. From the bedroom closet in the early mornings, the view is magnificent.

Which brings me to Friday morning. As the days shortened and Central Standard Time hit the clock, the roses began to fade. This past week, I clipped the last three reds and placed them in the middle of the kitchen table.

The table is the "cook table" from the Blonde's childhood. It is cherry and has my late (that word again) brother-in-law's initials carved in it. The small vase of three red Knock Outs are a stark contrast to the dark wood.

The last roses of summer, even in their beauty, are just as much a forecast of cold winter as *The Old Farmer's Almanac*. And for the record, *The Old Farmer's Almanac* agrees with my rose bushes:

"The Old Farmer's Almanac's long-range weather predictions for 2014-2015 are now available — and another teeth-chattering cold winter is on its way across the United States!"

The almanac's editor, Janice Stillman, adds:

"Colder is just almost too familiar a term. Think of it as a refriger-nation."

I like that term "refriger-nation," but the definition leaves me cold. (How's that for a play on words?)

Truth is my toes are always ahead of fading roses and *The Old Farmer's Almanac*. When I get out of bed on Labor Day morning, I put on two pairs of white socks instead of one. My toes know more about what's coming than James Spann and/or the National Weather Service.

The good news is I'll go back to one pair of white socks on July 4. The Blonde doesn't care for my white socks, but after all, July 4 is Independence Day.

Before that, there are countless days and nights in which we live in the shiver mode. Friday morning, the temp at our house was 24 degrees. Somebody on TV said it felt like 17.

I tried a third pair of white socks, but couldn't get my feet in my shoes.

But good news is the roses that die in the fall will be back in the spring. I don't remember an exact date, but around here I'd guess that will be sometime in April or May.

And again the view from the penthouse (closet in our master) will indeed be splendid.

I can hardly wait, but I know I'll have to. My belief and love of spring roses is considerably stronger than that of winter roses ...

FACES OF THE SOUTH

GHOST DOG? NO, JUST BLACKIE WAITING FOR UNCLE SAP ...

AUGUST 4, 2005

HAWK, Ala. – To paraphrase poet Sam Walter Foss, Blackie lives in a house by the side of the road, but he is no friend to man.

You see, Blackie's best friend passed away a year or so ago, and while there's a small doghouse at the pasture gate where Blackie and "Uncle Sap" used to ... oh, sorry 'bout that. An introduction to the main players in this little essay is in order:

Blackie: A dog – mongrel really – of indeterminate age and of uncertain ancestry who, most say, would be a Top 10 in any ugly contest. He'll take your food, but not your hand.

Uncle Sap: Christian name Willis Herren, Blackie's master since puppyhood. Also co-owner of the local sawmill and a man of considerable respect in the community until his death a year or so ago. He and Blackie were inseparable.

House: A small doghouse alongside Alabama 48, maybe a mile from Spratlin's Grocery in downtown Hawk. The house has the name "Blackie Herren" above the door and is where Blackie hangs out since Uncle Sap passed away. The house was built for Blackie by Ricky Spratlin, who operates Spratlin Grocery in downtown Hawk.

I first heard of Blackie and and Uncle Sap from Pat Harrington back in April.

In a letter, Pat told of a small black dog that lived beside the road in Randolph County at a pasture gate on Highway 48 south of Hawk.

According to the letter, the gate opened into Cut Nose Creek bottoms, where Uncle Sap kept beef cattle. Just about every day, he and Blackie would go check on the cattle.

After Uncle Sap died in January of 2004, Blackie took up vigil at their gate and has been there or in the vicinity since.

I didn't think all that much about the story, but others began to tell me about Uncle Sap and Blackie.

"Willis and Blackie would get in his pickup and go check the cattle every day," said H. E. Daniel, a coffee buddy from Woodland. "And Willis, he drove real slow, about 5 mph. When he got ready to turn, he'd turn, no signal, anything. You had to be careful if you were behind him."

H. E. also told me that all sorts of people wanted to take Blackie home with them, but couldn't catch him.

"He'll take food out of my hand," says Tommy Herren, a nephew, "but I wouldn't try to touch him. He might take a chunk out of my hand."

But when it comes to eating, Blackie is more accommodating. All sorts of people leave food and Blackie eats very well.

"One lady told me that when she takes her mother to Lineville to the doctor, they always buy two cheeseburgers for Blackie and give them to him on the way back," according to Pat's letter.

"I'm not going to call any names," says Tommy Herren, "but I had one lady come up here (to the sawmill) and tell me about another lady who goes by there with food, bread and stuff, throws it out and drives on.

"She said flies got all over the food and that wasn't good for Blackie. She said she always brought meat and 'I stay there while he eats.'

"She was really upset."

The upshot of all that is I finally went looking for Blackie, visited his house by the side of the road on at least four occasions. Never home, not once, and I kind of got a sneaking suspicion that my friends might be setting me up.

"Ghost dog" is what I figured.

But people kept telling me that they'd seen Blackie "just last Saturday morning, or maybe it was Friday morning, I'm not sure." Stuff like that.

Then, Wednesday night, Intrepid Ace Photographer Steve Gross called to say he had actually visited with Blackie and had several pictures he had snapped with his digital Canon EOS 1D.

He really did have a picture of Blackie ... or a reasonable facsimile he had transposed onto a photo of Blackie's "house by the side of the road."

It occurred to me that maybe Steve was in on the setup, but then I remembered Steve is not only a very fine photographer, but is also one of the better known baseball umpires in this area, and everybody knows baseball umpires are honest if nothing else.

So, I do believe in Blackie and I sure intend to get down here again pretty soon and maybe visit with him.

If Uncle Sap doesn't come for him first.

JOHN DEERE, EGGS AND WATERMELONS

AUGUST 16, 2015

ANY MAN who has three John Deere tractors, a John Deere mailbox, and grows watermelons as big as a city water tower may not exactly be a friend to man, but he's sure a friend to me.

One reason is I'm a graduate of John Deere University, which was located on my grandfather's farm, and I love watermelons. If you've never enjoyed a "fistbuster" while sitting under a pine tree on the edge of a watermelon patch, you haven't the faintest.

Truth is, you probably wouldn't know a John Deere if you hit one head on ... in a cotton patch, of course.

Lawrence Edwards, the guy with the John Deere mailbox and one of my Woodland buddies, came to the Waffle House (Oxford Exchange) this past week, He came bearing watermelons, tomatoes, peppers, and enough money to spring for breakfast.

OK, so you might say that's payola, but between friends, so what?

Besides, you don't step on another man's blessing, and when someone wants to give you something, it makes him feel good. Far be it from me to wipe out a good feeling.

Anyway, Lawrence is a man of the dirt if there's ever been one. Which means I almost knocked the eggs off my plate when he said:

"I've rented out most of my farm, decided I just can't do all that stuff any more."

In digesting this rather startling announcement (from a man of the dirt), a couple of things hit me. If he'd only rented out part of his farm, that means his divorce papers from dirt had not yet been signed. And that "can't do all that stuff" said he was still doing some "stuff."

I asked him how many cows he still had:

"Thirty five or so, just bought a new bull the other day."

I also asked him what he was going to do with his John Deere tractors.

"Just bought a new one the other day, a small one with an end loader. I had one I was going to sell, but decided to keep it."

Let me see now. Three John Deere tractors (not to mention the mailbox) and 35 head of cattle (including a new bull), and he calls that "retiring."

Which was exactly the prologue to the rest of the retirement story, that coming even before the waitress poured our coffee. You can quote me:

He ain't gonna do it. No Sir. Don't care what he says.

You say the name Lawrence Edwards rings a bell with you?

It sure could, like "The Egg Man From Woodland."

Which lets me tell you something I've told you before, that for 50 years Edwards had an egg route that sent him to local restaurants in Anniston five times a week in the good times. Five times a week dwindled to three or so as local restaurants faded in favor of chains. Like the Waffle House at the Oxford Exchange.

"I first came up here in 1950 and when I stopped it lacked just two months being shy of 50 years.. One of my best customers was the old Rainbow Inn, just down the road from here."

That I feel a kinship with Lawrence Edwards as well as a priceless friendship should come as no surprise.

We are of the same generation, kids who were born on the tail end of the Great Depression and grew up in the hard times of the rural South. It was a place and time where money was something people who drove big black Buicks had and we didn't.

It was a day and time where child abuse (as in slave labor) was not yet a crime. Had it been, I could have had my dad and a couple of uncles arrested and charged. They would have settled out of court.

And, as part of the settlement, I would have gotten my Uncle Freeman's John Deere tractor.

Thanks Lawrence ... and I'll see you next year in watermelon time ...

TWO OLD FRIENDS
ON A QUIET DAY

AUGUST 19, 2004

MILLERVILLE – It is doubtful either remembers the first time they met.

It was probably first grade. They've been best buddies ever since ... Class of '58 at Millerville High, both going to work for Alabama Power Company within a month of each other, both now retired.

Tuesday, on a day so quiet you can hear the padding of a stray cat beneath the shrubbery, they take notice of the shoulder-high weeds covering the football field at their old school.

"Looks like ragweed to me," offers the quieter of the two.

His buddy, the talker in the friendship, turns to look at the elementary wing of the abandoned Bibb Graves High School and Millerville Elementary.

"Built that grade school there when I was in third grade," he says. "Used to bring in coal with a scuttle, remember that?"

"Yeah," answers the quiet one.

"That gym, oughta give it to some church for kids to play in if they could get somebody to take care of it."

It was quiet for a second, then:

"Been some good basketball played in there," offers the talker.

"Got that right," his pal agrees.

A peep through the door window says the Millerville Bulldogs were, indeed, pretty good basketball players.

Two large glass display cabinets holding 57 trophies remain in the lobby. Two are for Alabama Class 2A State Championships, 1970-72.

"Who was the best basketball player ever at Millerville?" a bystander asks.

"He was one of 'em," comes with a nod toward the quiet one.

"Nah," was the reply. "The best ever was Richard Gortney. He was about 6-6 and could move. Hadn't been for him, they'd never won either of those state championships. He got a scholarship to Auburn, played a couple of years. He could have gone anywhere."

It was not Millerville's first glory.

"Back in the '40s, they beat Lanier — that's Sidney Lanier — in the state tournament," adds the talker. "Finished second. That was back when they didn't have but one classification."

For the former linemen for Alabama Power, the lights on the football field are of interest, too.

"Helped build that field," says the quiet one. "Climbed the poles, strung the lights. Everybody worked for free. Everybody."

"Must be 85-foot poles," says his buddy.

"I'd say 75."

Friends may argue, but not about 10 feet of creosote pole. Talk drifts to other subjects. Six-man football here in the '40s is mentioned.

After a while, the two leave and drive back to Ashland, stopping for coffee at McDonald's.

There is more talk of old Millerville High, of how it was to work for Alabama Power "when we were there."

After coffee, it's time to head out to the cattle barn for lunch, maybe even hang around for the weekly auction ... or maybe drift on home and take a nap before supper ...

OF 5-CENT COTTON
AND A WONDERFUL LIFE

APRIL 2, 2003

WADLEY – Dwight Hall will tell you he was 15 before he had a pair of dress pants to wear to church.

He can also tell you of cotton selling for 5 cents a pound, eggs for 10 cents a dozen, of wearing feedsack shirts made by his mother on an old Singer sewing machine.

He doesn't have to tell you about his good nature, his bubbling enthusiasm, his love for all things on God's good earth, nor that around here he is something of an icon ... a beloved one, at that.

"Have you talked to Dwight Hall?" is a question you hear when people discover a reporter is in town.

"Dwight's really something," comes with a shake of the head ... and open fondness.

"If I don't get or give 50 hugs a day, it's not a good day," says Hall, a chubby little guy with an impish glint in his eyes, in all ways sort of a reminder of what you expect a leprechaun would look like.

Don't believe me?

OK, next time you're here, stop in at Hall's Food Store on Main Street and see for yourself.

He'll be there ... just as he has since he bought the store back in '45 from the late Ray Parrish, who originally had hired Hall to "doctor chickens."

That was in 1940, which means Dwight Hall has been on this corner for 63 of his 82 years.

The thought that he was once a "chicken doctor" delights Hall.

"I was still on the farm," he says, "and had learned to doctor sick chickens. I had written to Auburn for some stuff. Anyway, Mr. Parrish was in the feed business and had put laying hens with several farmers around here. He asked me if I'd go to work for him, keep a check on the chickens."

He gave $5,000 for the store.

"I didn't have a penny, not one," he says. "I went to see the bank president, Mr. John Gibson. He asked if I thought I could handle it. I told him I knew I could.

"He said, 'I'll tell you what I'm going to do. I know your family's work ethic and honesty. I'm going to let you have the full $5,000; not even take it to the board, 'cause if I do, they'll want 10 percent down. I know you don't have it.'

"I was scared to death. That was more money than I'd ever dreamed of, but with the confidence he'd placed in me, I couldn't let him down.

"I paid it off $500 a year over 10 years," he adds. "That man made my life."

It is a life he wouldn't change.

"I've been up to Pigeon Forge and Gatlinburg," he says. "Been to Panama City on short vacations, but I've never been over the ocean. That's it."

His companion along the way had a lot to do with keeping near his roots.

Her name was Sara Edge. The two were married in 1941.

"She was raised on a farm right down the road from us," says Hall. "She was a beautiful woman and a beautiful person. One of the greatest Christian ladies I've ever known.

I've always said that if I could get to be 10 percent of what she was, that would be all I could handle.

"I would have never been successful in business without my precious wife. She was the hardest worker I've ever seen. I worked because I had to; she worked because she loved it.

"She died March 12, 1996, and I've had a hard time adjusting," he adds. "When you lose a great partner, it's a really hard thing."

The union produced two kids: Jerry, who is now in business with his dad, and a married daughter in Chattanooga.

The store is headed for a new facility just outside of town. It's open seven days a week, Sundays from 7 a.m. to 2 p.m.

Dwight Hall is there.

"I get an hour off to go to church on Sunday, but then I come back," he says. "I work six and a half days a week now, but I'll be 82 on July 12. I'll be a little more mature then. They're talking about me working seven days, eight hours."

Ask Hall if he ever thought he should have done something else and you get a quick answer.

"Not once," he says. "I didn't make much money then and I still don't, but it's been worth it. The things I have learned from my customers are precious.

"And I've never wanted to be the biggest supermarket around, just the best."

A vote here would probably be in his favor.

Then there is Hall's "ministry."

"I'm not a pastor, but I'm in a ministry," he says. "I can lift people up. They come in here, maybe down. If they will, I'll go with them to a private place and we'll pray.

"I'm serving God in a different way. We're all supposed to be in ministry, we all have some little job we can do. I think that's what keeps me going strong, I really do."

"Going" is an operative word if Hall can find the doors of a church open ... anywhere.

"I went to 35 revivals last year," he says. "I was saved at Beulah Congregational Christian Church when I was 15. It's still there, had a three-night revival last week. I went every night."

The move to a new, sprawling store out on County 33 is not one Hall anticipates.

"You can talk to Jerry about that," he says. "I've had a lot of wonderful years here and leaving is depressing. I don't know if I'll go or not, but they want me to."

Ask which way to bet on that and the grin and impish glint in his eyes reappear.

You know he's going ...

SALLY GRIFFIN: HANDS 'N' LEGS 'N' GOING HOME

SEPTEMBER 6, 2006

Come Friday, it's all over.

All those years of getting up at 4:30 in the morning and being on the job by 7, then heading home at 3:30, are finished.

It's time to go to the house and maybe just sit for a while.

Only problem is, Sally Griffin, in her 50 years at Anniston Sportswear, has never had a "sit-down" job. Getting used to that "sitting" may be difficult.

On her feet in the cutting room, on her feet in "stay front pockets" or as now in "mark waist," quick hands and sturdy legs have been her allies.

Thing is, Sally doesn't want to go home and sit. It's the doctors who are calling a halt, putting a finish to a job she's loved, one she doesn't want to give up.

But then, it's at least a minor miracle Sally is still at Anniston Sportswear.

There was a broken hip somewhere back in time and a hip replacement in 1994.

The broken hip came in a fall at a bread store.

"They put me in the car and I drove home," says Sally. "Then I got sick and had to go to the emergency room. Had surgery the next day, on a Sunday."

That would indicate a bit of toughness to go with the good legs and quick hands that have kept Sally on "production" at Anniston Sportswear for so many years.

("Production" is a form of payment. The more you produce, the fatter your paycheck.)

The hip replacement kept her from Anniston Sportswear almost five months. The rest of that record shows Sally missing work on only four other occasions in her 50 years. Two of those were for maternity leave.

"I've got two sons, two grandsons and two great-grandsons," she says with pride.

You do need good legs for what Sally does and "right now they're kind of giving out on me. That's why I'm retiring," she says.

"Sally doesn't want to go," says Marty Wade, plant personnel manager. "Since her job is production, she has to move fast to keep the work flowing to the next job. Keeping busy is what keeps Sally going. She's slowed down a touch, but she still makes production."

So what now?

"I'll stay home for a while and then get out and find me something to do," says Sally. "I don't know what, but ..."

Staying at home just doesn't get it for Sally.

"We lived in Lineville before we moved up here," she says. "I'd been working at Higgins Slacks for four years when we moved. My husband (now deceased) worked at Bynum and we moved up here because it was closer to his work.

"I stayed home from September to January and said, 'I can't do this, I gotta get out of here,'" she adds. "So I came up here and put in an application. Before I got home, they called and wanted me to come in the next day."

That day was Jan. 3, 1956.

She started in the cutting room at 75 cents per hour, minimum wage at the time.

"I started out in the cutting room," says Sally. "Then, for the longest, I was in re-cuts. For the past two years I've been in (waist) marking.

"It's all right," she adds. "I like the job and I don't like sitting at home. There's a lot of good stuff out here ..."

"We've had people to retire with 42 years and with 40 years," says Marty, "but never one with 50 years.

"I'm going to miss her," she adds. "Everybody out here is going to miss Sally. Everybody looks out for Miss Sally."

LET ME TELL YOU
ABOUT A MAN ...

JANUARY 28, 2007

L et me tell you a story about a man I heard about not too long ago.

You may know him, you may not.

It was really cold the night he was born, Feb. 18, 1917, and his mother said he was so small she was afraid he wouldn't live through the night.

Somebody later said he weighed just five pounds, that his mother put him in a box near an old-fashioned wood stove to keep him warm and alive.

She also had his picture made soon after he was born, fearful that her frail baby wouldn't live to be a year old.

But he did.

The middle child, I've always heard, is really a tough kid, and he was, in the words of his daughter, "the very middle child of six brothers and sisters."

So he lived.

His birth would not be his last courtship with death.

When he was 15, he stumbled and fell under a mule he was plowing with. The startled mule kicked the young boy in the head and he wound up at the old Garner Hospital in Anniston.

Doctors were able to staunch the blood pouring from the injury and he lived ... again.

Oh, there were such things as measles and whooping cough, chicken pox and runny noses, but he made it to manhood just in time to get in the middle of World War II.

He wound up in Laredo, Texas, where he and a team of mechanics inspected and repaired big bombers such as the B-24 Liberator and B-17 Flying Fortress.

On one flight check, the plane's landing gear wouldn't work and the plane did a belly landing, skidded to a stop ... and he walked away.

Death had been cheated a third time.

After the war he came home, got married, went to work at the Anniston Army Depot. He worked there for 30 years, but lost his wife to cancer in 1979, ending a 33-year marriage.

Then, in 1981, according to his daughter, "God blessed his life with a second bride ... Their blended families began a tradition of celebrating holidays together whenever possible."

But death would take one more swing at the man.

In July of '04, he and his wife were in a terrible automobile accident. Both were gravely injured; he was in the hospital two months.

On Feb. 18, he will be 90 years old, and I suspect the two families will get together for a very thankful birthday.

His daughter says, "If you ask the man about his experiences, he will say, 'The good Lord took care of Margaret and me. He's still blessing us daily. When bad things happen, you just have to keep looking up.'"

Oh, by the way, the man and his new bride celebrated their 25th wedding anniversary this past August, altogether numbering his married years to 58.

One other thing.

The man's name is James Vaughn Morris and he lives in Weaver ... in the same house where he and his first wife, the former Helen Wells, raised a son, Clayton, and a daughter, Elaine.

And I want to thank Elaine for writing this column for me today.

I hope you enjoyed it as much as I did.

PEACHES: 'WE'VE GOT THE PRETTIEST TREES ANYWHERE, BUT ... '

MAY 28, 2008

CLANTON — The "Peach Man" folded his hands atop the weather-grayed picnic table, looked at the old white farmhouse, and his first words were:
"Dad always said ..."

It's been years since "Dad" — Leon Easterling — pulled on his farmer's straw hat and walked into the peach orchards across the road, but his legacy seems richer with the years.

I visit here each spring, checking on the peach orchards that have, since 1952, sent fruit all the way across state to Anniston and Oxford for the palates of eager fans.

"When's the Peach Man coming?" is a refrain that begins in early April.

This year, as usual, there are stories before the asking.
Dad used to ...

"I can remember when we had three mules to cultivate this 67-acre farm," says Ken Easterling, the son. "I still have all the plows and the mule collars and that sort of stuff. He bought his first tractor in 1956, but only got a disc harrow with it. The rest we did with the mules."

The news is not that good, people.

In the beginning, Ken thought he was looking at a bumper crop.

"The peaches were in beautiful bloom," he says, "as pretty as you've ever seen. We've got the prettiest peach trees anywhere, but there's no fruit."

There is some, but a late cold snap did a hit and miss in Chilton County, but in Easterling's orchards, it was a lot of "hit" ... very spotty.

Dad used to ...

"He believed in black oil and bailing wire to keep things going," says Ken. "I'll tell you something. If you're going to make it on a small farm now, you'd better do things like that. And that's the truth."

Ken's first trip this spring is probably two weeks away.

"I'm going to have peaches," he said, "but it's going to be mid-June or maybe later before I get up there. The first load I get, I'm going to Anniston and Oxford. I need 250-300 baskets for a load. The other day, I picked five trees and got two baskets."

We walked into the orchard just to the right of Ken's boyhood home and got a first look at gorgeous trees with maybe a dozen or so peaches. In some cases, you'd find a limb with two mature peaches ready for picking, another three or four on the same limb, shriveled and withering, still a sickly green.

Dad used to ...

"Chevrolet pickups have been good to us. Dad bought his first Ford in '37 and people would ask him for a ride in it. He'd say, 'If you've got enough cat hair, you can ride.' Dad always called money 'cat hair' and that was his nickname, Cat Hair."

In all the years Ken has walked these orchards, he has to go back a long way to find a spring as bad as this one.

"It'll be our worst crop since 1955. I didn't see a single peach of any kind that year. I was 13 years old. We walked across the road, it was on March 15, and the peaches were already black. Dad thought it had probably killed the trees, too, but it hadn't."

That, alone, kept the Easterlings in the peach business. *Dad used to ...*

"I remember Dad would come in from the field and he'd kick those old brogans off on the back porch. Mom would have lunch ready. He'd eat, take a short nap, and get up and go back to work. People don't know what that is now."

Neatly placed among the Easterling orchards are rows and rows of tomato plants, 8,000 of them. It is a plan that the tomatoes will at least let the farm breathe a bit this year.

But Ken isn't so sure.

"It's hard to sell tomatoes to somebody wanting peaches," he says. "It just doesn't work very well.

"Some growers are doing fairly well," he adds, "but I just learned of a couple over at Maplesville who also thought they were going to have a good crop, but they're experiencing the same thing as I am."

So why does he keep on keeping on?

The answer is simple.

"You have to love it to do it," he says. "I just love to grow peaches."

Meanwhile, stay tuned. I'll let you know when the first truck leaves town headed your way.

OF FADED OVERALLS
AND ONE LEG

SEPTEMBER 21, 2006

BELL BUCKLE, Tenn. – He was wearing faded Liberty overalls, had one leg, a lived-in face, more hair on his face than on his head, and said he was from Nashville.

It was the first time, he offered, that he'd ever been to Bell Buckle.

But he smiled a lot and said that when he was a small boy he loved playing in the dirt "down in south Georgia."

Which, in sort of a roundabout way, led to what Jim Wheeler was doing in Bell Buckle. He was looking to show — and sell — his pottery (stoneware) to the hundreds of tourists who drift through here on any weekend.

"When I was a small boy in south Georgia, I played in the dirt a lot, good clay," he said. "I was always building forts and other things. I can't remember when I didn't want to do something with my hands. Clay lets you use your hands, lets you be creative."

A guitar picker with one of those voices you hear but won't remember was trying to draw a crowd, but Jim Wheeler's pottery was getting more attention than the guitar picker and his songs.

The pottery, some of it on a table in front of the Bell Buckle Press, the rest on the hood of an old Lincoln Town Car across the street, was getting most of the attention.

It was 9:45 in the morning and he said he'd already sold "five pieces since we got here."

It was a good beginning, and Wheeler was smiling ... big.

"My pottery is dishwasher-safe, oven-safe," he said. "You can eat off it."

He also pointed out that none of the 200 or so pieces he and his son had hauled from Nashville were alike.

For Wheeler, that's a point of pride.

"There are people who do production work," he explained. "They'll sit all day and turn out 50 rice bowls, all alike. I just can't make myself do that. My pottery is all inspiration.

"I don't have any drawings, maybe just an idea. I'll sit down with a lump of clay and go from there. I have a lot of bowls that are similar, but you'll never see two just alike."

Wheeler, who lost his leg in an auto accident "about 20 years ago," is (at 62) still a work in progress insofar as his pottery is concerned. While the pottery has evolved over the years, he has been in the wholesale and retail eyeglass business and also had a landscaping business at one point.

Along the way, he picked up a degree in graphic arts from Nashville State, has been president of the Preservation Plant Society of Middle Tennessee, and at present is "trying to sell real estate."

He also teaches, part-time, pottery in the Nashville metro school system for adult education.

"This past year, I've put on a drive to fulfill my dream of producing enough (pottery) to make some money."

Then, wistfully, he adds, "But if you do this to make money, you're never going to make big money."

Is there a story line here somewhere?

I think there is ... and it's one that is in all of our timelines ... hopefully: Somehow, somewhere, someday, we will eventually find where we are going.

I sure hope Jim Wheeler is about there.

MAE HARPER: OLD WASHTUBS AND PAYING THE RENT

AUGUST 3, 2006

TABOR ROAD – It's 9:15 Wednesday morning and Mae Harper already has made her rent.

Not bad, considering The Great American Yard Sale doesn't officially start for another 18 hours or so.

But Mae Harper has a prime spot, the corner of Tabor Road and Dutch Drive.

A huge water oak shades her eight tables, and in the early August heat (it's already 86), shade can be just as important as what you're selling. It will cause shoppers to linger a bit.

The parking is also along the road where Mae's $15-per-day spot is located. If you stop to shop here, you have to pass through Mae's "stuff" to get to the other vendors.

This is also the starting line — if you're heading north — for 450 winding miles of American trash or treasure, depending on just who's looking at what. The finish, if you and/or your wallet hold out that long, is Covington, Ky., just across the Ohio from Cincinnati.

"I was out here at quarter of six this morning," offers Mae. "I maybe should have come Tuesday. People are coming out pretty good. Sold two old galvanized wash tubs ($15 each), some glassware and a few clothes. I've already made my rent for at least three days. You get your rent made, you can sort of sit back and loaf.

"I like to loaf."

Read that again ... and then consider a couple of things:

1. Mae Harper has curly, white hair, but she doesn't look 80 ... which she is.

2. This is Mae Harper's 10th year working the yard sale. She also has a small shop in East Gadsden, works there five hours a day, six days a week, and then adds church twice on Sunday to go with her Wednesday night prayer meeting.

Oh, before she opens Mae's Used Clothing and Notions at 11 each morning, she's out at daybreak looking for area yard sales, doing some buying for herself.

So ... read again:

"I like to loaf."

With that, I can also tell you that Mae Harper has had THREE hip replacements, one neck and one shoulder operation.

"I've got a bad back, too," she says, "but you meet a lot of people with bad backs. So I don't guess that counts."

Quiet a moment, she adds: "Unless it's mine when it hurts."

Just getting her "stuff" hauled from East Gadsden to a mile or so up Tabor Road from Noccalula Falls, then getting it unloaded, unpacked and on display, is enough to make anybody's back hurt.

"You don't ever bring enough tables," she says. "Don't care how many you bring."

Under her dozen or so tables, I count 41 boxes of merchandise, all of the glassware carefully wrapped in old newspapers.

"My car is packed out, too," offers Mae.

A visitor mentions that if not careful, she could work up a sweat.

"If I start sweating, let me know," she replies, pointing to a blue lawn chair nearby. "I work about five minutes and then I sit about 15."

Having worked in a cotton mill, then a doctor's office, and outlived her husband by 32 years, why would an 80-year-old who likes to loaf keep this sort of pace?

"I do it for the pleasure," she says. "I enjoy it. It's a pastime for me."

But with a nice easy smile, she adds:

"It's for making money, too. I wouldn't be in it if not for the money."

Besides, as she puts it, "It would be a lonely life if I just sat around home and look at TV all day or look at the four walls.

"As long as I'm able, I'm not going to do that."

SOMETIMES THE HARD TIMES ...

JANUARY 21, 1996

MOBILE — Sometimes the hard times just won't leave you alone.

That's a line from a popular John Denver song of a few years back.

Not many 64-year-old black women are John Denver fans, but my guess is Florence Williams would say that pretty much is what her life has been all about.

Flo's Barbecue, opened just two months ago, is owned by Florence Williams.

Located three blocks north of Rousso's Seafood Restaurant, one of Mobile's finest, Flo's Barbecue is a dingy hole in the wall where just paying the monthly rent is chancy at best.

An evening meal at Rousso's can run in the $30 range, not counting certain libations in which you might also choose to indulge.

A barbecue sandwich at Flo's is $3.75. Her top entrée is a barbecue plate, four ribs, two side orders and bread for $6.25. Your drink is extra. Similarity with Rousso's ends right there.

Rousso's plays to a full house noon and night. I had a cup of coffee with Flo during the lunch hour on Wednesday. She had just three customers during the time we talked.

Retired from Scott Paper Co. after 27 years, Florence Williams is the mother of seven kids. "I've got 34 grands, 23 great-grands, and I'm raising one of my granddaughters," she said.

There was noticeable pride in the revelation.

There was quiet when she added, "I was divorced for seven years." And that her current husband is paralyzed.

All the kids, she says, have done well, including one by the name of Bo Wright who played football at the University of Alabama (1984-88) and more recently with a professional arena football team, the Tampa Storm.

A half-dozen or so color photos of Bo in action hang along one wall. They are the only bright spots in what is otherwise desperate deterioration. There are some things even fresh paint cannot hide.

But smiles help. And Flo smiles a lot— even as she recounts mounting troubles, including failure to obtain a business loan to "put this place in the shape I want to."

She opened on a shoestring, using her own money. She admits the string is about to break. In the two months she's been open, she hasn't taken out one dime for herself.

Why the gamble? Why not stay home with the company pension and the Social Security?

"My mother worked as a housemaid," she says. "She walked to work every day of her life, a mile and a half. She had been retired 18 months when she had a stroke and died. It came to me that had she kept on working, she'd never had that stroke."

She's upbeat, she's cheerful.

But she also admitted to the loneliness of the midnight "when I wake up and can't go back to sleep, wondering what's going to happen. I get to the point of crying, but the Lord says he will help me, and I believe that."

But what if this doesn't work?

What about 10 years from now?

What does she see for Flo then?

"I haven't thought that far ahead," she answers, "but I believe that I'll be where I want to be. If I don't make it here, I'll go and start some other kind of business. Or take care of some older person. I'm not going to quit."

You don't have to be a genius to know Flo's Barbecue won't be here six months from now, probably not even two. But you also recognize that in the inner strength of the George Roussos who built a success and that of Florence Williams there is a kinship.

The results simply have been different, which, if nothing else, proves again that life really isn't always fair.

For Flo, you wish that was not so.

ROGER KISER: IN HIS WORLD, A PLACE IN TIME

AUGUST 9, 2009

GOSHEN — This ain't Canton ... nor is it Cooperstown. But tucked away on a quiet country road in the southern end of Cherokee County there is Roger's Museum.

Step inside the 10-by-12 storage building tucked up against Carol Kiser's back porch and, in a blink, you're down "on the plains at the Loveliest Village" or maybe at "The Ted" in Atlanta waiting for Chipper to come to the plate.

You're in Roger Kiser's world ...

It is a world of baseball caps and baseballs and photos and jerseys and autographed photos of former Auburn coaches Pat Dye and Terry Bowden.

The Dallas Cowboys hang out here, too, in a locker of their own standing in a corner. On a shelf along with dozens of baseballs and some 330 caps hanging on the wall is a bronze bust of Abraham Lincoln. John Wayne sits "tall in the saddle" here, too.

It is a wonderful place in time.

It is also the world of a 52-year-old with Down's Syndrome. His name is Roger Kiser, yet a "kid" who now uses a cane to get around.

The museum was born a couple of years ago in the hope Roger Kiser's bedroom might still be in there somewhere beneath all his memorabilia. Before the move, his bedroom was wall-to-wall.

Standing with me as Roger proudly lifts and replaces, with care, his "museum" exhibits, there was this from his mom Carol:

"This has been his world since he was about six years old."

Later, sitting at her kitchen table and watching her son come through the living room, there is more ... from the heart.

"When Roger was born, the doctor waited three months to tell us he had Down's ... He was my first child and one of the doctors encouraged us to put him in a home and give me a new baby.

"Thank God we didn't take his advice. Roger has been such a blessing in all our lives. He forces us to be better people, to look at what really matters in life.

There were more children, a daughter, Lynne; and a son, Kevin.

Kevin, a Clay County commissioner, talks about his "big" brother, too.

"Growing up with Roger gave me the best playmate I could have. He was always home with me, he was always ready to play, and he was older and more mature in most ways.

"But then slowly, over time, I became the older brother. I became more the protector and less the playmate. I learned about taking care of those less fortunate from my experience with Roger."

In that is a message, one that says no matter who we are, what we are, we contribute in some way, good or bad, to the world in which we have been placed.

Look up Down's Syndrome and when you think about the life expectancy of Roger Kiser the day he was born, Dec. 7, 1956, you'll understand what I'm trying to say.

There are photos of family here, too.

Roger picks up one and points to a white-haired man in a tan suit and says:

"That's my daddy, right there."

He lost his father, J. T. Kiser, two years ago.

Kevin talks about that:

"My dad showed his love for my brother to the end. Some of his last conscious acts were to assure Roger that he was going to be okay without him. He went to great pains to make sure his passing would not be stressful for Roger ...

"He took Roger places and stayed on his feet a lot longer than he should have ..."

There's more from Mom:

"I've spent most of my life with Roger. He has been with me almost every day since 1956. He is a joy to me. He loves to meet people, he loves to go to gospel singings, he loves the Gaithers. And he loves to go buy groceries ...

"He loves Spring Garden basketball and Auburn football and the Dallas Cowboys and the Braves and a million other teams."

Spring Garden Panthers?

Roger went there in the first grade. There is, just inside Rogers Museum, one of those decals with a huge pawprint and the legend, Panther Country.

I'm blessed in that I have been to Roger's Museum, I've seen the joy in his life and warmed in his infectious smile, have heard the love in his mother's voice, in his brother's words.

I hope, in some way, so have you.

GEORGE SMITH

THOSE WHO SERVED

THEY WERE OUR SOLDIERS, OUR HEROES

NOVEMBER 10, 2005

Just a picture on a table, just some letters Mama saved,
And a costume brooch from England, that has on the back
engraved,
  "To Eileen, I love you, London, 1943"
But she never heard from him again, and he never heard
of me.
                                          — The Statler Brothers

Friday is Veterans Day.

I'm not a veteran and I'm thankful for that.

Sometimes I joke that if I had ever gone to war, I'd have been shot in the back.

But when I see old men and listen to their memories, when I see a movie such as "Saving Private Ryan," when I attend a funeral and look at a flag-covered coffin and hear the melancholy strains of "Taps" drifting over a quiet cemetery, I know one thing:

I am thankful for veterans.

And I feel a loss when I think of those who did not come home, but are buried on foreign soil, the place marked by a simple white cross, a Star of David if Jewish.

We are the dead. Short days ago
We lived, felt dawn, saw sunset glow,
Loved and were loved, and now we lie
In Flanders fields.

That is from World War I. In 1921, an American soldier, "known but to God," was buried in Arlington National Cemetery.

In 1958, two more "unknowns" were interred, one from World War II, one from the Korean War. An "unknown" from the Vietnam War was buried in 1984, but no longer is there.

A 24-year-old Air Force pilot, Michael Blassie, was identified by DNA tests in 1998. His family moved his body home to St. Louis.

I had four uncles who saw combat in World War II.

Three were sons of Houston and Hattie Smith of Ohatchee.

The fourth was a young soldier out of West Virginia's coal mines who met and married my mother's baby sister while at Fort McClellan. A few months later, he was at Bastogne in the Battle of the Bulge.

I've told you all of that before, probably will again, but they were my heroes and I loved them dearly.

One was "Uncle Larn," who wrote my grandmother a V-Mail in 1943. He was in England at the time.

He, too, was in the Battle of the Bulge. He was with Patton's Third Army, sent to relieve the encircled 101st Airborne at Bastogne.

Time has claimed three of my uncles; the fourth is 81 and doing just fine.

He is still my hero and best friend.

And when I see flags fluttering and hear "Taps," I remember my grandmother and I hear, in my mind, the hurt of wartime love in:

And the war still ain't over for Mama,
Every night in her dreams she still sees,
The young face of someone who brought her,

Silver medals and sweet memories.

Friday is for all our veterans. Remember that for a while, won't you?

THE NIGHT THEY BROUGHT
THE BODIES

APRIL 23, 1995

MARSHALL, Ind. — Riley Tidwell, a retired truck driver from Gallatin, Texas, leaned into the gathering twilight as if he could really see the mountains of Italy, as if it were again April 18,1945.

The second-story veranda here at Turkey Run Inn was quiet except for the sound of Tidwell's memory recalling the night his captain, Henry T. Waskow of Belton, Texas, died.

Ernie Pyle, World War II's best known correspondent, wrote a column about the incident. The column is considered perhaps not only Pyle's finest work, but of any other war correspondent, too.

It was an incident and a column which made Tidwell, a 6-foot-5 runner for Waskow, forever a part of the war's lore and something of a folk hero. Upon his return from Italy, Tidwell was shuttled around the country as a spokesman for war bonds, rubbing elbows with the rich and the famous in the process.

"Pyle and the captain made me," offered Tidwell, tugging at his straw cowboy hat.

It was a making Tidwell was unaware of until he was rotated home.

"I'd never heard of Ernie Pyle," says Tidwell. "I didn't know who he was or anything about him until I got off the boat (back) in the States."

There never was an official meeting during the short time Pyle spent with Tidwell's outfit, Company B, 143rd Reg., 36th Infantry Division. He's pretty sure Pyle never met the captain either.

"I was with the captain the night he was killed," says Tidwell. "I was his runner and was real close to him. It was like losing my daddy when I lost him.

"We were in the mountains around Casino," continued the lean Texan, seemingly oblivious to his two listeners. "We had been in reserve and was moving up the mountain, advancing when it happened."

For a few moments, peering into the gathering darkness of April 18, 1995, you had the feeling Riley Tidwell was no longer there on the veranda with you, that he was, indeed, back there in another April evening with his captain.

Finally, he spoke again ... and again very quietly:

"He must have heard it coming," said Tidwell. "I remember he pushed me and another guy down. The last words he said was, 'Get down.'

"He probably saved our lives, but he got it anyway."

A piece of shrapnel the size of an apple had torn into Waskow's chest.

Suffering from a bad case of trench foot, Tidwell finally made it back down the mountain to a cowshed in which Pyle and several soldiers were spending the night.

"I remember somebody saying Ernie Pyle was in the cowshed, but that's it," says Tidwell. "I knew there were several soldiers in there, too."

Tidwell's concern was for his dead captain and there is a "rest of the story" not contained in Pyle's famous dispatch.

"I remember him (Pyle) standing beside me and asking about the captain's body and would it be coming down the mountain," says Tidwell. "I didn't know who he was, but I explained to him that the men who carried supplies up to the troops each night on mules would collect the dead bodies and bring them back down when they returned.

"But they didn't bring the captain down that night. I waited. I waited the second night and they didn't bring him down then, either."

The third night, Tidwell did what most any good soldier would do for his captain.

"They kept the mules out in an apple orchard," says Tidwell, with just the touch of a smile. "I knew where the captain's body was. I stole a mule and went up on the mountain and got him."

Bringing the body back down in pitch blackness was no big problem.

"It was a pretty wide trail," says Tidwell, "and the mules had been up and down it enough all you had to do was hold to the reins and let the mule find its way."

It was the Germans' practice, however, to randomly shell the trails at night, just on the off-chance of nailing a load of supplies or reserve troops moving to the front. It was such a shelling that caught up with Tidwell on the way down.

Shrapnel tore into his left wrist, which has required seven surgeries since the war ended. A gash near his left ear required 15 stitches.

"I was pretty bloody, but the wounds were not that serious," continued Tidwell. "I don't remember anything about getting down the mountain, but I remember hearing somebody saying, 'Here's Riley and he's got the captain.'"

Waskow's body was "laid in the shadow beside the low stone wall," wrote Pyle. "Four other bodies were placed beside the dead captain's."

"All the men in the cowshed started coming by and saying something (to Waskow)," recalls Tidwell. "After they did that, I knelt beside him and sort of rearranged his uniform. Then I said goodbye and walked off, too."

Silent another moment, Tidwell said:

"That's the way Ernie finished the story, but I didn't know anything about it until ..."

As Tidwell's voice trailed into what was now a dark Indiana evening, he pulled a handkerchief from the pocket of his jeans and, pushing his glasses aside, wiped at obvious tears.

"Every time I read that column or talk about it I get emotional," he explained.

Just before he left, Tidwell had one other thing he wanted to say.

"This is the last one of these I'll probably get to attend," he said. "Two weeks after I agreed to come here, I was diagnosed with cancer. It's in my stomach. It's terminal."

That came matter-of-factly, without emotion.

And then Riley Tidwell walked away ... again.

PAUL TIBBETS:
THE FIRST PALE HORSE

NOVEMBER 4, 2007

And when he opened the fourth seal, I heard the voice of the fourth living creature saying, Come. And I saw, and behold, a pale horse: and he that sat upon him, his name was Death.

— Revelation 6:7

When I heard the news of Paul Tibbets' death Thursday morning, my memory clicked to a mild September morning on a quiet street in Columbus, Ohio.

From a hospital bed by a large window, Paul Tibbets, with wavy, graying hair and still handsome in his 92nd year, can see the shadows in his backyard, shortening as the sun climbs toward noon.

Like the shadows in his yard, Tibbets' time is near.

I have come with a good friend, Mike Harden, Columbus Dispatch columnist, to the bedside of the man who dropped the first atomic bomb on Japan. We have food for Tibbets and wife Andrea. Harden does this frequently.

"He should be dead," Harden tells me, "but he just won't quit."

Mike holds Tibbets' hand, talks with Andrea. It is somewhere in there that I notice a large painting on the wall, one Tibbets can see from his pillow.

It is of his plane, the Enola Gay, emerging from a cloudbank over the Pacific. It is early morning and the low sun plays shades of gold and pale to the underbelly of the clouds and of the Enola Gay.

It is the only memento connecting the man and the long-ago flight that killed 75,000 and more on Aug. 6, 1945. I can also see the Tibbets' living room, dining room, kitchen, and a long hall leading to the bedrooms.

Like the den, there are no remembrances of that time, of the years he rode B-17s in bombing raids over Germany, no medals, no pictures.

"He was such a simple, simple man," Harden told me by phone Saturday morning. "No pretense. He loved Bob Evans strawberry cream pie and his best friend was a tool and die machinist, but he was a fine machinist. The one thing Tibbets couldn't tolerate was mediocrity in anything."

It was somewhere in there that the working title, *Pale Horse*, of a book Harden is writing about Tibbets came to mind. In Harden's words:

"He rode the first pale horse of the nuclear age ..."

Harden told me about Tibbets' granddaughter, Kia.

"She was raised in this house," said Mike. "She knew he was famous, but once said, 'To me, he was just my grandfather.'"

On the way out the door, Harden pointed to a tree with, "That's a weeping Japanese cherry tree. I don't know what it means, but nothing was done without Tibbets' approval."

Finally, this from the Intelligencer/Wheeling (W. Va.) News-Register:

"Beyond any reasonable doubt, the use of the atomic bombs saved more lives than were taken by them. Even if those like Tibbets who understood that clearly are passing from our midst, Americans need to remember that."

From 11 years old to now, I have.

'OLIVE DRAB' AND 'ALWAYS MY HERO ...'

MAY 14, 2008

Drill sergeants can cry ...

At least I know one that can.

Her name is Kitty Moore, and before she became the Veterans Service Officer for Calhoun County, she was a drill sergeant at Fort McClellan.

That was yesterday's life ... 250 brand-new recruits every seven weeks.

In today's life, she and the two other women in the local office are helping mend those once-raw recruits who are losing to time, who have given limbs to service, who have Agent Orange in their past, who walk a thin line between a getting-by today and an uncertain tomorrow.

For Kitty, whose mom and dad were also military, it is emotional ... very.

"I bleed olive green," she admits, "or you might say olive drab. I love the Army. And I can't help but get emotional because you know what we're doing for these veterans now is nothing compared to what they've done for their country."

The walls of her tiny office, tucked away in the rear of the county administration building, is a gallery of those veterans. Pictures of uniforms, of their wives and husbands, their

99

children, in some cases their parents, decorate the tree. Then there's the box of tissue on the desk that I first noticed when I asked her to tell me the saddest story she knows.

"I've got to have a Kleenex first," she said, reaching for the box.

Even before the story, there were misty eyes ...

"The saddest case I ever handled was a young man who was in the first Gulf War, Desert Storm and Desert Shield. He was in a helicopter crash and burned over 90 percent of his body. He has really bad burns on his hands, face and neck.

"He sat in here and talked with me that first time and I won't ever forget what he said.

"He said, 'Mrs. Moore, the only thing that bothers me about this is I'm not a soldier anymore.'"

Silent a moment, Kitty Moore added:

"I told him that he would always be a soldier ... and when he comes in here, I tell him he's my hero."

Then there are the happier times.

"Happiest is when you have a widow come in or an elderly veteran who is having a really hard time and is not aware of what the VA can offer," says Kitty. "You file a claim and they get their money every month. It helps to pay for their medicine, for their care, for anything they want to do with the money.

"It gives them a new lease on life."

Another pause and, "I guess I've gotten a hundred thank you cards."

Certainly there will be a few more.

The day I visited, a 10-inch stack of folders, each holding a pending claim, sat on her desk. Another stack was nearby.

"All of us do the same thing," she adds. "There are days that, between the three of us, we may have 40 to 45 people in here. The office is full, they're sitting outside in the hall. And that's not counting the enormous number of phone calls we handle."

The "three of us" includes Cecelia Talley, administrative assistant; and Roselyn Westbrook, assistant service officer. It is worth noting that Westbrook's son is currently with the Army in Iraq.

Without going into detail, Kitty's list of what her office can deal with for the veterans ranges from service-connected compensation to applications to state and federal VA nursing homes. All told, 17 items are on her list.

"We don't get into legal issues or personal conflicts with family, but if a veteran has a need, he should contact us," she says. "We don't turn anybody away. Even if we don't have a claim here, we do everything possible to help. If a veteran comes and says he's hungry, there are food banks. And there are certain social-service organizations, the Commission on Aging, Department of Human Resources ..."

Bottom line is, if her office can't help, she knows where to look for that help.

And it's not just the aging, either.

"Right now we're losing an alarming number of veterans who were exposed to Agent Orange in Vietnam, who have residual illnesses from that. We have some very sick veterans. And we have some veterans coming back from Iraq who are really hurting.

"It's very sad."

That it is personal and not just case files is found in a scraggly "memory" tree sitting on the office counter. It was once a Christmas tree.

"We always decorate," said Kitty. "We got it out, but it was so ugly, we said it couldn't go anywhere. We put our heads together and decided use it as a memory tree.

"We've got obituary notices on it, veteran names, what war they served in, branch of the military, pictures ...

"We need a bigger tree," was an assessment as she studied the tree with one of her "clients."

Only for Kitty, who had an arm around Hubert Craft, "client" is not a fit. Her "people" does.

"It is gratifying to help a veteran file a claim and see the benefits come to fruition.

"But one of the saddest aspects of this job is helping a veteran who has a terminal illness caused from a service-connected disability and then processing a claim for burial benefits when they pass away.

"I feel that we have taken a journey with them and their family members ... I feel that we have a bond with our veterans ..."

THEN THERE WAS ONE TO
BELIEVE ...

JULY 2, 2006

BOSTON — Joseph is tall, has a yellowing moustache that muffles his words, wears a big cowboy hat, and says he is from Minnesota.

Dan is 40, says he's from Scotland, and is heading for Chicago in a week or so to put his "doctorate in divinity to work."

Arthur is 58, says he's a fine carpenter, and is from just down the road, Waltham, Mass.

The three have one thing in common.

They are homeless veterans and home, at the moment, is the Northeast Homeless Veterans Shelter here in Boston.

Downtown, the old gray building that once housed a bank now can provide more than 300 men (and a few women) with beds for a night, for a week, for whatever it takes to, hopefully, move them back into mainstream society.

Friday, with a fellow columnist, I listened to each tell a story.

I had a bit of trouble believing Joseph.

"I've been working for The Lord for the last 25 years," he said, and then he talked about how the worst place to be homeless was Duluth, Minn.

"I've seen it 30 below," he said. "Step outside and you'd freeze."

He also said, in so many words, "Nobody cares about you. You can walk out there right now and die and nobody cares."

I believed that.

Looking at his boots, there was this:

"Boots are the only thing you can keep today," he offered. "You can heel and sole boots, but everything else you throw away."

Then there was Dan, a stocky sort with a quiet voice and a steady eye.

You won't believe what has happened to Dan in his 40 years ... wife and child killed in a car wreck; mother, father and sister killed in a plane crash.

That one sort of spun me around, but I can't really tell you he was stringing us along.

Arthur didn't claim to be working for The Lord, nor did he claim a degree in divinity. He just up and said he is a drunk, that it started in high school.

He also dropped out of school in the 11th grade, joined the Army, and went to Vietnam ... twice.

"When I got out of the Army I threw my uniform in a trash can and came home," he said.

And turned into a drunk.

"But I think I had a few problems with alcohol before I went into the service," he said. "I think that's what motivated me to go in, to try to stay dry.

"But when I came home it was like being in a time warp. The peace movement was in full swing ... I went into a downward spiral."

Since 1990, there have been substantial periods of sobriety ... six years, three years, 18 months.

The last time he fell, "three things happened. The war in Iraq broke out, I had a brother to die and my divorce became final. I haven't been able to put anything together since.

"In retrospect, I think it started with Desert Storm. I was by myself and I just sat there and watched it and drank."

His last drink, this time, was May 16 ... less than two months.

There probably will be a next one, too ... a month or so, maybe a couple of years.

But maybe, just maybe ...

ON A QUIET HILL ... UNKNOWN ... UNKNOWN.... UNKNOWN...

SEPTEMBER 27, 2006

BEECHGROVE, Tenn. – You drop down off I-24 and swing left under the Interstate. The fried cornbread at the Bell Buckle Café is just 12 miles away.

But an image of an old cannon atop a hill just as you turn flickers in the mind's eye. A quick U-turn brings you around a curve and up a small hill to an old Confederate cemetery.

It is a gorgeous day in middle Tennessee, low 80s with a gentle breeze ruffling the leaves of a giant hickory that shades the heart of the cemetery. Small tombstones, weathered to gray, stand silently in two long rows across the brow of the hill.

There are 53 of them. And, as I walk slowly between the tombstones, I read:

Unknown Confederate Soldier ... Unknown Confederate Soldier ... Unknown Confederate Soldier ... Unknown ... Unknown ...

There are 49 unknowns. Only four bear the names of the dead beneath the closely mowed but ragged grass.

One reads:

Private William T. F. Pike
Hillard's Company A

Second Alabama Legion CSA
1842-1863
Another reads:
In Memory of
Charles Henry Johnston
Company F, 4 Ky. Inf. CSA
March 27, 1832 April 3, 1863

They are side by side. You wonder if they knew each other, if they died together. You wonder how well — or badly — they died.

Pike and Johnston were killed in the Battle of Hoover's Gap. They, along with the others, were gathered from scattered spots along the battle line and re-interred here in 1865.

Standing in front of one of the unknowns, for some reason a line from an old Johnny Cash ballad comes to memory:

The battle will rage in the bosom of mother and sweetheart and wife,

Brother and sister and daughter will grieve for the rest of their lives.

Forty-nine unknowns, on a quiet hilltop in Middle Tennessee; 49 who had mothers and sweethearts or wives, 49 who never went home, 49 who never had a mother or sweetheart or a wife to place flowers on their graves.

But it is utter sadness that the 49 unknowns here in Beechgrove Confederate Cemetery are not so much as a grain on a beach in the numbers across America, around the world, who are so entombed.

In reading about the Battle of Hoover's Gap, I ran across this:

Tread lightly, 'tis a soldier's grave,
A lonely, mossy mound;
And yet to hearts like mine and thine
It should be holy ground ...

— The Soldier's Grave

After a while, I walk down the hill, get behind the wheel, and head toward Bell Buckle, but thoughts are not of fried cornbread. My thoughts are, instead, of something I've often pondered.

Dear God, why is it that old men are allowed to start wars ... and young men die?

Why?

FAITH

LET'S SING A FEW
OF THE OLD HYMNS

JUNE 7, 2015

"Some glad morning
"when this life is o'er,
"I'll fly away ...
"To that home on
"God's celestial shore,
"I'll fly away ..."

It is the fifth Sunday in May and tradition at Blue Mountain Baptist is being observed ... singing, eating, and no preaching.

Not a bad deal really, even for Pastor Rev. Truman Norred. He loves to eat and has had a week off from poring through the fine print of his Bible in search of a message for a graying flock that is a lot closer to the finish line than to the beginning.

Truth is, Brother Norred also comes equipped with a razor for humor and he seldom passes up a chance to lay my miscreant ways before the entire congregation.

Sunday was an example.

We had been out of town for two weeks and Brother Norred dutifully welcomed us home and then:

"I knew George would be here 'cause he loves to eat."

For one of the few times in our relationship I think I bested him. From the fourth pew from the back, I raised my hand with:

"Best part is we don't have to listen to any preaching today."

In fairness to Rev. Norred, I have him at something of a disadvantage. As a man of the cloth, he has to pull his punches. As a member of a fourth estate that ranks somewhere behind Congress and Obama in respect for right and truthfulness, I have no such restraints.

With the foreplay out of the way, meet:

— Patricia Brown, who comes with a guitar over her shoulder and a voice that can bust a brown jug.

— Lafette Brown, who also comes with a guitar over his shoulder and can wrap real warmth in a Southern gospel song.

— Terry G. Parris, who comes with a mandolin and a voice that quietly blends with Patricia and Lafette.

— David Morris, who comes with a banjo, a guitar, and a fiddle and also quietly blends with the other three.

For near an hour, we sat and listened and I was carried back to the years of country music on the front porch after supper. I suspect most of the others felt the same way, comfortable and happy to be at Blue Mountain Baptist on the fifth Sunday.

The finale?

"To that land where joy will never end,

"I'll fly away.

"I'll fly away, oh glory, I'll fly away.

"When I die, Hallelujah, by and by,

"I'll fly away ..."

We stood and sang along, clapping hands and a few did a bit of wiggling ... if you get my drift. For a fleeting few moments in a church far too large for a dwindling membership, I thought, "Old country meeting time."

In that were memories of way back, when the small Baptist church at Pleasant Ridge literally rocked when Jot Cobb led the congregation in "I'll Fly Away."

It is one of the great mysteries of my life as to why "I'll Fly Away" is NOT in the Baptist Hymnal. It's not. Go check it out.

So much for the hymnal selection committee. I've always maintained that the only songbook a church really needs is the one Tennessee Ernie Ford used.

"I come to the garden alone,
"While the dew is still on the roses."

Ernie sings that to me quite frequently out in my barn.

There is also a memory of my early teens and the heat of Sunday mornings in August at Oak Bowery. The memory is of Virgie Hearst, our pianist, ripping through "The Lily of the Valley."

"He's the Lily of the Valley, the Bright and Morning Star,
"He's the fairest of ten thousand to my soul ..."

"Miss Virgie," who was one of my teachers at Ohatchee High School, also rocked as she swayed from side to side on her bench.

The windows were open, of course, and I'm still surprised someone with a Sunday morning hangover didn't walk in from off the road and answer the altar call.

I was one of Miss Virgie's "pets" in school and I still think about her a lot.

And sing to me the old hymns when you tune up "Give Me That Old Time Religion ..."

A TIME OF PREACHING 'N' DIPPING

SEPTEMBER 13, 2015

Stories you may have heard before ... but not today.

Somewhere in my "stuff" there's an old, small, black-and-white photo of a country preacher wearing a white shirt. His sleeves are rolled up to his elbows and he is waist-deep in a country creek along with seven of the "unwashed" who are about to be "washed."

The country preacher is my grandfather, the Rev. George D. Cobb, Sr. He was a quiet man who dipped a bit of snuff every now and then, but was something else when he stepped into the pulpit at tiny Pleasant Ridge Baptist Church. To put it another way, my gentle grandfather could chase pagans and infidels and agnostics with the best.

He was Jimmy Swaggart before Jimmy Swaggart was a gleam in his daddy's eye.

The times I sat and listened to him can't be counted. I do remember thinking I'd like to meet one of those infidels. They sounded like fun. 'Course I knew not to mention that to my grandfather.

Oh, one other thing.

He wasn't against throwing in a few unkind words about those Methodists down the road.

Sprinkling just wouldn't get you to heaven like an old-fashioned dip in a cold creek could.

So what got me on this?

Memories ... of other preachers who preached their way through my life.

My grandfather was the first, and his very best friend was also a preacher, the Rev. Arthur Haynes.

The Rev. Haynes was blind, but had a big, thick Braille Bible.

He was also a great storyteller. I spent a lot of time in his lap walking with Daniel in the lion's den, with Jonah in the belly of the whale, with Moses leading his people out of Egypt.

From there it is a skip of a few years to boyhood, like 12 years old or so, and the back bench at Oak Bowery Baptist Church.

The pastor was the late Rev. Buford Johnson, a tall and lanky man, who got my attention one hot Sunday night when he pointed his long and bony finger with:

"Remember, you're just one heartbeat from eternity!"

Buford said that a lot, and I'd grab my chest to see if my heart was still beating. After about a month of that, I walked down the aisle to redemption, frankly because Buford had, quite literally, scared the hell out of me.

When I was 20, I figured out He was offering me a pretty good deal so I asked Buford for a second washing. I can still hear his words as I gasped for air:

"George, if this one doesn't take I don't think there will be much hope for a third."

Over the years, I can't count the number of preachers who made my socks smoke. There was a bunch of them and, mostly, they were pretty good.

In recent weeks, I've been exposed to no less than three. My pastor, Truman Norred, had hip surgery and had to take to his recliner for a bit. In his stead, I got the Rev. James

Cohorn and the Rev. Bob Ford. Cohorn and Ford are former pastors at Blue Mountain Baptist.

I like to listen to all three, but I'm not sure the Rev. Jesse Barksdale isn't number one. Jesse is the pastor at Cedar Springs Baptist Church and, to be honest, I've never heard Jesse preach.

But Jesse, who knows trees and all that ails them, has been keeping a 50-year-old maple alive, if struggling, in my backyard.

I planted the tree, a mere sapling, when we moved here. Over the years, there has been some question as to which is number one with me, God or that tree.

But to quote the poet Joyce Kilmer:

"Poems are made by fools like me, but only God can make a tree."

Since God made my tree, I guess he is number one ... and I really hope he will be a little tolerant of my sometimes backsliding ways.

Whatever, get up out of your chair and head for church. That's where I'm going.

I have this feeling ...

OAK BOWERY: FOR THOSE OF US FOR WHOM THE BELL TOLLED ...

APRIL 19, 2009

MIDDLETON — The old "new" church sits in a dipping curve on a piece of what was once the main road to Ohatchee.

The new "new" church sits up on Alabama 144, a straighter and quicker road from U.S. 431. It is a highway that skirts my hometown of Ohatchee on its way to Alabama 77 and, just beyond, to Neely Henry Dam on the Coosa River.

Those are just a couple of changes around here since back in my natural prime, when I was early into my career as a "back-bencher" on Sunday morning.

The old "old" church, Oak Bowery Baptist, is where on a hot Sunday night in my 13th year, I walked down the aisle and declared I was ready to give my "heart and soul to my savior, Jesus Christ, Son of God the Almighty."

Standing in the churchyard this past week, watching Chris Clark and his crew pull an old and rusting bell from its tower, there were more than a few memories.

There is that long ago night, a night of Liberty National fans, sweat-circled armpits and the Rev. Buford Johnson in the pulpit.

He is tall and lanky, his body is already showing signs of the rheumatoid arthritis that would claim his life at a much too young age. The Rev. Johnson, one of the great country preachers of any time, is winding down his sermon ...

"Remember! You're just one heartbeat away from eternity ... each and every one of you ... one heartbeat ... one heartbeat."

In making that point (which he does on a weekly basis), Brother Buford swings his good right arm toward the brethren and waggles a long, bony finger. On this particular night, there is little doubt he is pointing directly at me.

Grabbing my chest just to be sure my heart is still beating, I head down the aisle and into his welcoming arms, to the man who had, quite literally, "scared the hell" out of me.

Thing is (to get this on the record), a few years later, after I had finally reached the age of accountability, I realized he really was offering me a pretty good deal, the result being Brother Johnson had to "dip" me a second time.

Recently, standing by a young Shannon Mullinax, who was working a long boom — ever so gently — to haul the old 800-pound bell out of the tower and to the ground, there are memories.

They are of the four days I was up there, in March of 1952, with my dad. We are building the steeple and topping it out with the tall white spire that still gleams in a bright sun. The remembrances are good.

But it also came to me that even back then I was more than a little crazy. It's farther up there in the sky than I remembered. But heck, nobody else would go up there with B.H. (best darn carpenter since you know WHO), and they were willing to pay me $1 an hour. Dad said I could skip school.

I did. And while the bell is headed for a new tower up by the new "new" church, I'm not sure I'm all that ...

But that's not a story. I don't have a vote in the comings and goings and doings of Oak Bowery Baptist Church. Still, it is my home church and ...

There is another memory of the old "old" white-frame church that I was in the night Brother Buford wrestled with Satan for my soul.

The congregation, somewhere along about 1951, decided the old white church had to go, that a new one — brick and all — would take its place. The decision was not unanimous.

Mr. Charles Goode, a deacon for over a half-century, spoke strongly against the move. Basically, what "Uncle Charley" said was:

"This is my church. It's the church I want to be buried in."

Uncle Charley got his wish.

The week they removed the pews and the piano from the old church in preparation for demolition, Uncle Charley left us.

The pews were moved back, services for Mr. Charles Goode, deacon and beloved husband of Rhoda Goode, were held. The pews were removed again. Demolition and life went on.

For the record, "Uncle Charley," whose baby son Monroe was my best friend, is buried on the side of the hill beside the old "new" church. He is buried there not only beside "Aunt Rhody," but with two other wives who preceded him in death.

It was not long after we moved into the new "old" church that a couple of young men, on a Sunday night, flipped their car in taking the curve in front of the church a wee bit too fast. Everybody, of course, ran outside to help. To weep and wail, too, if called for.

The young men were not hurt (they will remain nameless here), but one matronly lady jumped in front of one of the miscreants with:

"Young man, y'all should be in church!"

Swaying a bit on his feet (I suspect some "recipe" was involved), the miscreant peered at the lady with:

"No ma'am, we should be in hell ..."

For the record, the old bell made it safely to the ground. It will be restored, installed in a new bell tower "up on the hill," and will once again toll out Sunday-morning welcomes to the community.

A "back-bencher" never becomes a deacon, but on my way home, I had the thought that I sort of knew how "Uncle Charley" felt way back there in '52.

DOT: START WITH
THE LITTLE THINGS ...

OCTOBER 19, 2003

FRUITHURST — Granddaddy preached, Momma played the piano, and "Dot" has just finished 45 years teaching Sunday School to the "juniors" here at Fruithurst Baptist Church.

For Dorothy "Dot" Skinner, being in the Lord's service sort of comes with the genes.

"When I was growing up," says Dot, "I was carried to church. Not like today when some people just send their children to church and don't go themselves.

"My grandfather, John Patty, was a preacher, so I grew up in church. Church is very important to me."

Then there was Momma, Lonas Skinner, who played the piano at Fruithurst Baptist for 50 years ... a half-century. A few years ago, shortly after her passing, the congregation had a day in Lonas' honor and dedicated the Fellowship Hall to her memory.

Which brings into play the 45 years Dot has taught Sunday School to the children of Fruithurst.

"Jim (Rev. James Owens, pastor) says I've been teaching 45 years, but I don't know. I know I wasn't much more than a kid myself when I started teaching, but I felt it was important. Children need to learn the Bible."

Owens, himself once a member of her class, is a fan.

"Her knowledge of the Bible is astounding," says Owens. "She has been true in her teaching, always dependable, a big asset to the church. Our youth will be missing something good."

Dot always wanted to teach the young people.

"I always felt if I could help one child live a better life, just one, it was worth it," says Dot, sitting in a back pew of a church where she has been a member since her 13th summer. "I think maybe I have. I know I haven't been successful with all of them, no.

"But I never stopped with teaching just the Bible. I think children need to learn other things, how to behave in church, how to treat other people. In order to be a better person, you have to start when they're little ... from the ground up."

She may have taught her last Sunday School class, but the kids still belong to her.

"Oh yes," she says. "I still feel they're mine. I can still tell them to sit down and be quiet if needed."

One thing she said as I was about to leave, you need to hear.

"I really don't know why you're here," she said. "I'm not much of a story, never done anything important. I guess I was just raised to go to church and that's what I've done."

Not important?

A good guess is some four generations of "kids" who came through here on their way to adulthood would disagree ...

GARRY BURNS: OF FISH AND BREAD AND FAITH

FEBRUARY 1, 2006

"I don't believe you can scare somebody, beat somebody, drag somebody, force somebody to the Lord, but you sure can love somebody to the Lord and that's what He did in my life."
– Garry Burns, pastor, Center of Hope

Garry Burns took his first drink when he was 11.
I didn't ask when he pulled the first whiff of marijuana into his lungs and he didn't volunteer.

But he knows when he had his last drink, knows when the enduring love of his grandmother, a close friend, and a tiny baby brought him to his knees and into the arms of his God ... Dec. 6, 1992.

The grandmother was Nona Gober.

"She instilled something in me very early," says Garry Burns. "She worked seven days a week to provide for us, but she always let us know who was taking care of us. She told us it was the Lord."

The friend was (and is) Wayne Lee.

"I had worked with Wayne in all the clubs and bars around here," says Burns. "until he gave his life to the Lord.

He kept coming by and telling me that he loved me and that God loved me."

The baby's name was Nick. He is now 16.

"I was sitting at home and I was drinking," says Burns. "I was holding my son, 9 months old. I won't ever forget this: I was looking at him and my life was flashing by ... and I didn't know what I had to offer him. I thought, 'I can't be a daddy to him because I can't take care of myself.'"

Seated behind his desk at the Center of Hope on Bynum-Leatherwood Road, Burns is silent for a moment before adding:

"I had hit rock bottom. If this was all life had to offer, I didn't want to live.

"But that day, holding Nick, I accepted the Lord into my life. I didn't know what was happening, but I knew something inside of me had changed. And I knew it was something better than what I was living."

From that day, from a grandmother and a friend and a small baby, Garry Burns has been reaching out to help others who, like himself, have lived wasted lives of alcohol and drug abuse ... and, frankly, some problems with the law.

No fewer than 50 of those men, ages 18 to 52, now live at the Center of Hope in four-man bedrooms on the second floor. On the first floor is a 350-capacity sanctuary where Burns preaches his message of faith, hope, and redemption on Thursday nights and Sunday mornings.

Down the road in Eulaton, there is a house where eight women now live, women with the same problems as the men at the Center of Hope. Over the hill from the Hope building, construction is under way on a facility that will house 50 women.

There is a waiting list, just as there is for the men.

Those entering the Center are asked for a 12-month commitment.

"We call it a discipleship training school," says Burns, "a place where people that have been lied to can learn the truth and start depending on the Lord instead of depending on the things of the world that they have grown dependent on.

"While they're here, they are fed, housed and clothed, and attend classes and counseling. They work in our thrift stores, on the buildings, on the site, whatever. It's a sowing, a putting of something back."

For the first 10 weeks, you leave, you don't come back. After that, there's a 48-hour pass, another phase allows one day per week away from the Center to work ("Make a little money," says Burns), and in the fourth phase of their stay, they can work full-time.

"It is in that phase, the last three-and-half months, that we help in job placement, help them get their lives back on track, help establish a home so that when they walk out that door, the whole world won't fall back on their shoulders," says Burns.

There are successes, there are failures.

Burns speaks of that.

"We have folks who have gone forth and are now living full lives," he says. "And we've had folks who left and got caught back up in the world.

"But God spoke to my heart and said that what time they're here, a seed is sown and it will be watered and given increase."

The path to here, for Burns, led through Parkwin Day Spring, a non-denominational church not far from the Center.

It was there that Burns, with his friend at his side, accepted Christ, it was there he became a minister, it was there that he pastored for the first time. And it is here that Parkwin Day Spring has become the Center of Hope.

"I love being here," says Burns, "being a part every single day of something special happening in the lives of these men and women, seeing God restore families. It is really something to see a small child come through those doors that hasn't seen their mother or daddy in a while and jump in their arms. You know that there is hope that a family is being brought back together.

"There's no greater feeling. It's amazing how God has multiplied the fish and the bread out here."

DEAR GOD, I CAN ... THEY CAN'T

SEPTEMBER 1, 2005

The swirling reds and oranges move onto my TV screen Sunday afternoon.

The images have a name ... Hurricane Katrina.

She's gone, I'm not ... and I'm still mesmerized by the images out of New Orleans and from along the Mississippi Gulf Coast.

And I know that I am blessed ...

They hurt, they mourn dead, and search for missing.

I know where mine are.

They're hungry and thirsty.

I'm not.

They have no homes, I do.

I have a job, their jobs are gone.

The blonde says, "Sweetheart, supper's ready."

Lord God, how long before they will hear that again?

I can turn on a light, settle in an easy chair, read a book, watch the Braves, and doze off.

They can't.

I can turn off the light, get in a soft and dry bed, touch the lady already there, and drift into peaceful slumber.

They can't.

I can wake up in the morning, turn on the coffee pot, take a bath, poach an egg, toast bread.

They can't.

If I need bread or milk or grape jelly, I can run over the hill and get it.

Their store is under water ... or gone ... or being looted.

I have ice for my tea, sweetener if needed.

What would they give for just that?

I have dry socks in a chest, a clean shirt in the closet.

They don't.

I have a comb, a toothpaste, and toilet tissue.

They don't.

Gas out on the highway is up to $2.63 and I'm ticked.

They'd pay twice that ... if they still had a car.

If I have a toothache, Dr. Finley is my rod and staff and will comfort me.

Their dentist is ... where?

I can pick up the phone and call an ambulance if I'm hurting, a policeman if I'm threatened.

They can't.

They are defenseless.

I can pick up the phone and reach out and touch my son, my grandsons, or just a friend.

They can't.

My street is one of family homes and shady trees and green lawns.

They wander a rubble-choked street in Biloxi and cry.

They sit on freeway overpasses, above the flood, and wait for someone to come and help, to take them to fresh water and a clean bed.

I wait in line at a drive-thru for a cheeseburger and fries and gripe at the wait.

They have waited days for a cold sandwich from the Red Cross.

I can escape their misery by turning off the TV.

I can't.

They can't.

They are, in every sense, prisoners of Katrina.

Dear God, help ... them ... and keep safe those of us who are safe.

They are not.

BENNIE LEE: 'GETTING HERE WAS THE HAND OF GOD'

APRIL 5, 2006

MELLOW VALLEY — It's been 15 years since Bennie Lee Yates saw the bottom of a whiskey bottle.

God put Bennie on his knees one night in the Yates' living room and basically told him a couple of things: You're losing everything, and you're going to die if you don't leave the bottle alone.

It's been three years, give or take a bit, since God put Bennie on his knees again, basically telling the one-time Southern Union basketball star that he needed to teach history at the new Mellow Valley Christian Academy and throw in a bit of God's love along the way.

This past week, I caught Bennie on his knees again.

This time he was kneeling by eighth-grader Rachel Wright's desk, helping her with a history assignment.

"Getting here was the hand of God," says Bennie. "When they first called, I didn't want any part of it. Then, Donald McCullars (MVCA principal) called one Friday night — I wasn't here — and talked with my wife.

"When I came in, Sonja told me what he'd said, about what kind of school they were going to have here. I went to bed with that on my mind. He called back the next morning.

129

"We talked about 10 minutes. I asked if I could pray over it. I told him I'd call him back by 3 that afternoon."

With a smile, Bennie adds, "But when I hung up, I knew what I had to do. God had put it on me."

Included in the new job was a substantial pay cut.

"Yeah, it was a pretty good cut," says Bennie, "but Sonja was for it all the way — she's always seen things in me I couldn't see — and even though I took a pay cut, we never missed a lick.

"The Lord has blessed us."

Maybe this is what the Lord had in mind way back when Bennie, shooting lights out for Southern Union and planning to be a coach, minored in history as something of an afterthought.

"I've always loved history," he says, "and I'm old enough (50) to remember things happening that we're now teaching.

"God gave me a gift to remember a lot of things about where I was when certain events happened, like when JFK got killed. I know exactly where I was. I was in study hall at Daviston High School. We played Rockford that night in the Coosa County basketball tournament. I remember wearing a coat my cousin gave me, a hand-me-down.

"Another thing I remember sharing with them was the old duck-and-cover stuff they came out with in the '50s. In case of a nuclear strike, you were supposed to get under your desk and cover your head with your hands and arms.

"The kids really got a kick out of that," adds Bennie, chuckling.

"The kids" are from the seventh grade through the 12th.

In other words, Bennie is "it" in the history department at Mellow Valley Christian Academy, a pre-K-through-12th in its third year, born when Clay County opted to close Mellow Valley High School.

"To me, this is all about the kids," he says. "And I get to interact with them, and that's my Christian witness for them. Sometimes as grownups, we forget these are kids and that we were their age at one time."

Walking out into the spring sunshine, Bennie looked around at the graveled parking lot, the old deserted Mellow Valley school next door, at a few kids heading for the low, flat-roofed building where he teaches, and gave me one final thought as I headed for my car.

"This is the only job I've ever had where I want to get up and go to work," he said.

ON SUNDAY MORNING,
A BABY CRIED

OCTOBER 9, 2003

BLUE MOUNTAIN — Something unexpected happened during Sunday morning services at Blue Mountain Baptist Church.

A baby cried.

Nobody seemed able to recall the last time that had happened. Everybody agreed it was good.

"When I heard the baby cry, it startled me for a moment," one lady said. "But it was really good to hear. I wish it happened every Sunday."

We are, to be honest with you, a "graying" church of dwindling membership. Babies at Blue Mountain come in their grandparents' wallets, and photos don't cry.

There was another snapshot from the past, too. It took longer than usual to pass the collection plate; four ushers instead of two were needed to work the aisles.

What brought the crying baby and the full collection plates was our 100th birthday. A lot of people who found salvation at Blue Mountain came home for the occasion. The sanctuary, which seats 300 or so and normally has 40, maybe 50, for Sunday morning services, was near full.

It was a wonderful day, bittersweet, too, in some ways even melancholy. It is a truth that a "graying" church does not have a very bright future. In case you missed it, East 22nd Street Baptist held its last service a couple of weeks ago.

But our dwindling membership has not yet caught our beginning.

On July 31, 1903, a meeting to determine if a church was needed in Blue Mountain was held. In a second meeting, 23 "were presented for membership," and the first service was held in the "Twine Mill Chapel" on Aug. 9.

You can read "cotton mill chapel" there in that our church was just that, a mill village church. "We" left the Twine Chapel in 1906, moving into a big (for the time) white building just across from the mill. The present sanctuary was built in 1963.

My time here goes back to that second church and the Rev. Buford Johnson, a great man of God whose life was cut much too short by crippling arthritis. In fact, Buford was such a fine preacher he managed to baptize me twice.

I've told that story before, how at age 13 I answered the altar call because he flat out scared the hell out of me. I can still see Buford up there in the pulpit at Oak Bowery (near Ohatchee), pointing a long, bony finger and intoning, "You're just one heartbeat from eternity."

The finger was always pointed directly at me, enough so that I'd grab my chest to check my heartbeat.

The second time, at Blue Mountain, came in my early 20s, when I finally figured out he was, indeed, offering a better deal than the one I had.

Among those who "came home" Sunday was his wife, Louise.

That, too, made it a wonderful day ...

And for one Sunday morning and for one more time, we could say, "We had a really good crowd today for preaching."

And a baby cried ...

WILD TURKEY, DEER
AND THE RAPTURE ...

JULY 19, 2009

The blue sign bordered in yellow reads "Randolph County 33."

There are other ways to get from here to Wadley, roads of long straights and gentle curves.

But for me, it's Route 33 ...

Why?

I'm glad you asked ...

At the risk of being something of an "old geezer" here, one question for you:

Do you remember when you were 16 and driving a car was fun?

On today's highways — the interstate comes to mind — you aim and point and try to avoid the 18-wheeler from Cummings, Ga., on its way to Waco, Texas ... or wherever.

On Route 33, you actually get to again drive your car ... setting up for a curve, drifting through the bend, pressing just enough gas to be accelerating coming out, and ...

OK, enough ...

Except there is more to Route 33 in Randolph County than a winding 14-mile drive to a quiet river town and an early breakfast at Bonnie Wilkinson's Country Kitchen.

Especially if you do it along about "just-past-good-daylight."

It can be a spiritual thing ...

On a last drive, four deer cleared the highway in like three bounds.

Further along a big doe ambled across, apparently with no buck in chase.

Twice, wild turkeys strutted across the road, necks for all the world remindful of a clock pendulum ... back and forth, back and forth.

On a last drive, I met exactly one car in the 14 miles.

On a last drive, I saw one person, a lady in a housecoat, tugging a garbage can to roadside. That one person had me wondering if the rapture had occurred and she and I were the only ones left.

On a last drive, I saw exactly one plastic bottle and one Styrofoam cup. People along Route 33 can not only spell "t-r-a-s-h," they don't "do trash," either.

On a last drive, I slowed to wonder at the ageless beauty of Macedonia Baptist Church ... white clapboard, tall clear windows, steeple stretching into the early morning ... Sunday School, 10 a.m., Preaching at 11, the Rev. Jones, pastor ... I didn't get his first name.

On a last drive, I slowed for old, abandoned stores, one with a rusty Texaco sign out front. I wondered how much the owner had on his books when he finally closed the doors.

On a last drive, I looked at three-bedroom bricks from the '50s, weather-beaten farmhouses from the '20s and '30s with honest-to-goodness front porches. I wondered who lived there, who had lived there, what had their lives been like.

On a last drive, I looked at piney woods and overgrown pastures where cattle had once grazed. Pulpwood is the future along Route 33 ... and I wondered when last cotton or corn grew from spring planting to fall gathering.

On a last drive, I passed through communities such as Forrester's Chapel, Level Roads and Louiana. You'll not find any of those on the map, but people along Route 33 know where they live.

On a last drive, I drove 14 miles without seeing a Walmart, a McDonald's or a traffic light.

On a last drive, I had a conversation with Him because every time I ride Route 33, I get this feeling that this is where God hangs out when he's looking for a quiet place to sort of catch His breath ...

Can't say as I blame Him, not one bit.

IN REMEMBRANCE

OF PEOPLE WE MEET AND REMEMBER

APRIL 28, 2005

People pass through our lives all the time ... every day. Sometimes they linger for a while, becoming friends. Others leave as quickly as they came, mere acquaintances who may have enriched our lives, may have taught us something of value.

Those remain with us as remembrances, others fade as though they never existed.

This morning, I have a remembrance, a very lovely one.

I can't tell you when first we met, but it was maybe three weeks back and she was sitting across from me at the breakfast table at Autumn Cove, an assisted-living facility in Choccolocco Valley.

My aunt is there and I had dropped in for breakfast.

It is a wonderful thing for me that I did.

The lady I met that morning had lovely, sort of wavy, silvery hair. She had blue eyes that lived, a smiled that loved, and a quickness of mind that played easily with good humor.

Her name was Mabel Crabtree Young and she told me she was 91. I told her: "You're kidding me, no way!"

It was the beginning of a wonderful time, sitting across from her for an occasional meal, listening to her talk of her three sons, of a husband who is 84.

"You robbed the cradle," I said.

With that delightful laugh that could light dark, she said, "Well, he just kept on after me, and I finally said yes.'"

She was diabetic and told me about that, too. And she told me that her husband was in a nearby nursing home.

"He has Alzheimer's," she explained ... with a poignant sadness I would not hear again.

Then, one morning, she wasn't there.

I waited for awhile, thinking she was merely running late, before I finally asked.

"She had a small stroke," I was told. "She's in the hospital."

Daily, I would hear, "She's stable," or perhaps, "We haven't heard anything today."

Tuesday morning I was told that "Mrs. Young died. It was in the paper Saturday."

After a while, on my way back to town, there was a remembrance of the morning she found out that I write for the newspaper.

"Oh, good," she exclaimed, beaming. "I've never had my name in the newspaper. Why don't you put all our names in the paper? We'd love that!"

There were two other ladies at the table. I wrote down the names, told Mrs. Young, "I'll do that one of these days."

I still have the names in my notebook, but Mabel Crabtree Young, 91, of Oxford, made the paper before I got around to doing it for her.

Her obit appeared Saturday morning.

I'm saddened by her passing, I'm sorry she didn't get to see her name in the paper. But even more, I am thankful Mabel Crabtree Young passed through my life.

Her remembrance is a precious one ...

IN MY MEMORIES OF CHARLIE

SEPTEMBER 29, 2013

From the window I can see a white cat strolling across the patio.

In the early-morning light, the cat heads for the hedgerow. I set a cup of black coffee on the desk, turn on the computer, bring up The Anniston Star, go to the obituaries.

It's a ritual as common as plain flour, the beginning of another day on Arrow Avenue in Saks. The first obit is short. On the monitor screen it is just two lines, 26 words total.

I look at the name, briefly, and move on ... but suddenly the name registers. I lean back in my chair. A slow sorrow is growing inside me. I read again:

Ohatchee — Services for Mr. Charles A. Ward, 80, of Ohatchee, will be announced by Chapel Hill Funeral Home. Mr. Ward passed away Friday at his residence.

I knew the rest of Charles A. Ward's going away would be in the next day's paper. It was, telling those who read that he had married, had been preceded in death by his wife, Betty. It said they had two daughters, Cindy and Terri, and that he was a "native of Calhoun County and a lifelong resident of Ohatchee where he graduated from Ohatchee High School, he was a member of Victory Baptist Church and had served in the U.S. Army."

Then, watching the day come ...
Memories of Charlie ...

I'm not sure when Charlie came into my life. I think I was in the ninth grade and he was a year ahead of me, maybe two. I've forgotten that, too.

I do know Charlie fell in love with a girl in our class, a sort of sultry, pouty beauty by the name of Betty Jean Martin. She had dark hair, greenish-blue eyes, and spoke her mind without apology. You never had to guess what Betty Jean — we called her by both names — was saying.

That, to me, was sort of neat. In addition to her looks, that may have been one of her attractions to Charlie. From the day they began courting until she went away a few years back, Charlie always knew exactly where he stood.

And the standing must have been pretty good because Charlie just about always had a nice smile on his face. And when he mentioned Betty Jean in conversation, there was warmth in just the way he said her name..

Charlie, at one point, was a center on the football team, but he never made All-County or anything like that. He was just a solid kid who showed up for practice every day, did his job on Friday night, and held hands with Betty Jean.

Memories of Charlie ...

He was not — as the obit said — a "lifelong resident" of Ohatchee, but other than the time he spent in the Army, he never got far from his hometown. For several years, he and Betty Jean lived on Saks Road, just over the hill from our house. Their two daughters, in those years, were in the same age range as our two sons. Like their parents before them, they were classmates.

There was, from time to time, a visit. It was usually a quiet supper, a time of keeping up with each other's kids, wondering whatever happened to so-and-so, have you heard from them lately, things like that.

Memories of Charlie ...

The last time I talked with Charlie was at the Lenlock Walmart, maybe six or seven months ago. It was after he had lost Betty Jean and I asked how he was doing.

He said he missed Betty Jean a lot, but didn't get all weepy. And we talked a while. He told me about his kids and grandkids, I told him about my son and grandsons.

As we parted, he turned back and, with that old "Charlie smile" from other years, said "I'll see ya."

Sadly, that didn't happen, but that is also not unusual in the course of human affairs. Good intentions too often are just that ... intentions.

Memories of Charlie ...

The blonde, a few weeks back, ran into Charlie at a doctor's office.

In the conversation, Charlie pulled pictures of his daughters and his granddaughters out of a shirt pocket and did a nice bit of "proud" in showing them off.

That is just one of many things that said Charlie was all about family.

But in his 80 years of being a good and decent man, I suspect Sept. 21 was the only time Charlie ever got his name in the paper.

The "Charlies" in our lives deserve more than that.

But one other thing is Charlie was one of my heroes in the tender years. I can't tell you why. He just was.

GOAT: 'SHE WAS THE PRETTIEST THING I'D EVER SEEN'

SEPTEMBER 5, 2002

The obituary in the newspaper said that visitation would be from 6 to 8 p.m.

When I arrive at 5:45, the family is already receiving visitors.

B.C. "Goat" Henderson is sitting on a couch, near the open casket where Bessie rests. She is dressed in red, looking very much at peace.

Two of B.C.'s daughters are sitting beside their father, one is holding his hand, the other has an arm around his shoulders.

He looks up, takes my hand, and says, "I'd have had her 67 years had she lived 'til October."

The visit is short.

There's not much you can say at such times. You exchange a few words, express your support, say, "Call me if I can help." That's about all. You move on, others are waiting.

When I leave, at 6, the line is down the chapel aisle, into the lobby, and out the door.

In that simple summation of the end of a life, I think, is one heck of a tribute to people such as B.C. and Bessie Henderson.

She was 83 when she died, he will be 90 later this month.

The memory of when I first met the two comes easily. When I learned she was just 16 when they married and he was 23, I kidded him about "robbing the cradle."

"Saw her at a ball game," he had told me. "I was playing, she was watching. She was the prettiest thing I'd ever seen."

Those who know B.C. will tell you it is no surprise that the two met at a baseball game. The man loves baseball, always has, always will, and played in the industrial leagues in our town well into his late 50s.

The baseball was for fun, the living for a growing family (there would be three daughters, two sons), came from one of Anniston's many cotton mills, old Anniston Manufacturing on West 11th.

Bessie was there 36 years, B.C. put in 47.

The work was not easy, but there was security in the regular paychecks.

And there was a closeness in the mill village that transcends the years, a time and place B.C. and Bessie's oldest daughter, Mary Frances, remembers with warmth.

"It was a wonderful place to grow up," she says. "We were close, we played together, went to school together, went to church on Sunday."

And Bessie, above all, was saving, very saving, says her daughter.

Enough so that when the mill closed in 1977, the Hendersons had left the mill village for a nice three-bedroom brick on a big oak-shaded lot just south of Oxford.

The retirement was good, too ... family, grandchildren ("Mother loved her grandchildren," says Mary Frances. "She had nine."), gardens and canning, church, good friends.

In the years I knew them, Bessie was quiet, even a bit reserved. But you sensed that she was the strength, the anchor ... especially in her husband's life.

Certainly, that seemingly endless line of friends who moved slowly past Goat for a few words and to look at Bessie in her red dress said this was a special lady ... sort of like all the mothers we hold in all our memories.

And I suspect B.C. will tell you she's still the prettiest thing he's ever seen.

I WISH I HAD WRITTEN THAT ...

OCTOBER 17, 2010

COLUMBUS, Ohio — He was a son of the Midwest, a liberal to the core, but he loved country music and Ernie Pyle's writings.

Somewhere along the way, he became my best friend.

And then, sometime Wednesday afternoon, between lung cancer and pneumonia, he left me ... much too soon.

Oh, one other thing.

Mike Harden may have been the best newspaper columnist in America, a trade he plied for years at the Columbus Dispatch. And, oh, how his words could sing.

Just a simple line could grab you and make you say, "I wish I had written that."

Let me play this one:

"Democracy can be found at the Woolworth's lunch counter."

But it was the country music, the old country music, that turned a 1985 bet into a band of two brothers.

The love of country music came from his mother. From one of his columns:

"Her pleasures were small, her wishes were simple: a set of bunk beds for the room in which six small children slept, a new hot water tank. Nothing fancy. She knew 50 ways to

*stretch hamburger, a folk remedy for every common malady
and all the words to Hank Williams' songs."*

It was in the country music we first bonded ... at a columnists gathering here in Columbus in 1985.

On a bus ride back from an evening function, we sat together by chance, and when the others broke into song, we broke into how much each knew about country music.

In what I considered "Yankee" arrogance, a bet was made ... and I put his $20 in my pocket, moved to the front of the bus. Never, even unto his finish line, did I give him a chance to get his money back.

But the ties became close.

At yearly conventions, we were a foursome with perhaps a couple of ever-suffering wives. And there were personal visits, he and Debra to the mountains of north Alabama, the blonde and I to the flatlands of central Ohio.

Mike and I spent an awful lot of time listening to Willie 'n' Waylon 'n' Hank. We also spent considerable time deciding the fate of the nation.

Once, filling space in the conversation, I offered, "Mike, it's amazing all the stuff I know that doesn't mean diddly-squat."

His reply was classic:

*"Smith, let me tell you about journalistic knowledge. It's
like maybe 30 miles wide and a half-inch deep."*

His liberalism was born of his mother, too. That came in something he once told me:

*"In my mother's living room, there were three pictures, one
of Jesus, one of Franklin Roosevelt, and one of John L. Lewis.
I never really knew in what order they ranked with Mom."*

Another bond was our football teams, his Ohio State Buckeyes and my Alabama Crimson Tide.

On one trip to their home, he presented me with a Buckeye T-shirt. To his surprise, I wore it to supper that night. On our last trip, we gave him and his wife Alabama T-shirts. They wore them to supper that night.

A quiet-spoken person, there was a sensitive side to Mike Harden you read in his words, but seldom saw in person.

A story ...

In a first marriage that produced two sons, he and his wife decided they wanted a daughter. In Mike's soul were buried memories of orphaned Vietnamese babies he'd seen as a combat medic with the Marines.

Annie, who gave Mike a grandson and a granddaughter, came from there as a small baby.

There is more to that story, from Annie's teen years.

Mike, on his own ticket, returned to Vietnam in search of Annie's birth mother. Often he expressed regret his search was futile.

Then there is the one story, close as we were, that he told me of his Vietnam tour, how a flip of the coin saved his life, took the life of his best buddy.

"When we manned an outpost, a medic was required to be there, too. This night, we flipped a coin to see who would go out, the other going the following night."

I'll be a while forgetting a voice trailing into silence ...

"The outpost was overrun. Everybody was killed."

Memories of Mike Harden run long in mind and heart.

Space runs short ...

Thank you for listening ...

SURELY GOODNESS AND MERCY WILL FOLLOW ME

SEPTEMBER 21, 2000

TALLADEGA – The small in memorial pamphlets they pass out at funerals always carry a Bible verse on the inside.

The one handed to me Tuesday afternoon had the 23rd Psalm.

As I listened to the ministers eulogize Amy Haney, I kept reading the final verse ... over and over:

Surely goodness and mercy shall follow me all the days of my life:

and I will dwell in the house of the Lord forever.

For Amy's sake, I sure hope so.

If ever anybody deserved a break, a good helping of goodness and mercy, it was and is Amy Haney.

Certainly there was no goodness and mercy in the heart of Thomas Lee DeLancey the morning of Jan. 22, 1999, when he fired a bullet into the back of Amy's head.

The bullet turned a very beautiful young woman, a former cheerleader at Lincoln High School, into a quadriplegic ... instantly.

Listening to the ministers talk about her great courage, her grace, her dignity, I remembered the first time I met

Amy. It was in a Gadsden hospital where she had been since the shooting. She smiled when we were introduced, she was smiling when I left.

After leaving the hospital that day, one of the things I wrote about Amy was:

"You want to hold her in your arms and make her whole again."

That was impossible.

But that was also the day I met her aunt, Sheila Estes. And of all those now mourning Amy's death, I doubt any feel the pain of her farewell any deeper than Sheila.

To put it bluntly, Sheila dedicated 20 months of her own life to her niece. To provide some measure of quality in Amy's life, Sheila began looking for options.

She found options ... an in-body breathing system, a special wheelchair.

She also found out she needed $100,000. And between her job and at least two trips each week to the hospital to see Amy, Sheila raised that money. She did it through fundraisers. She also established *"For Amy's Sake"* on the Internet.

The e-mail Amy received really meant a lot to her, says Sheila.

In fact, Amy spent most of Friday, Sept. 1, re-reading those e-mails.

Then came the beginning of the end.

The next day, Sept. 2, Amy suffered a seizure.

"After that she was mostly in a coma," says Sheila, "but she had fleeting moments of recognition. Once she opened her eyes and looked at her brother Troy and said 'I love you.' There was another time they said she called for me, but I didn't hear that. I'd just left her room and was standing outside in the hall."

When someone dies, you hear things like "We come to mourn the passing of ... and to celebrate the life of ..." "Now in paradise" is mentioned a lot, too.

Intended as a comfort, those are also words of our faith.

Sheila Estes was clinging to that faith Tuesday afternoon.

"It's a comfort to know she's not suffering anymore," said Sheila, fighting tears. "It's a relief to know she is not restricted now in any way."

But of even more comfort would be that Thomas Lee DeLancey had never happened, that Amy would someday have married and had her very own Amy ... and lived happily ever after.

Sadly, life is not always a fairy tale.

WHO DID YOU SAY IT WAS?

JANUARY 22, 2006

They are everywhere, the white crosses alongside the road.

Some are draped with artificial flowers, others stand naked in time-weathered whiteness.

The crosses are silent, but they speak ... of death, of where someone died, of life gone in the split of a second that it takes for an automobile to die, too.

On U.S. 431, south off I-20 to Hollis Crossroads, there are three of them. Two are along the twisting, mountainous climb that tops out at the Cheaha Country Store.

I am a frequent traveler along that stretch, and when my foot is light and I'm in no hurry to get where it is I'm going, the crosses are sobering.

I slow down but don't stop.

I wonder who died and why.

Was a curve too sharp for the speed, did someone bet a pass on the yellow line and lose, was it icy or was it raining? Or was it just a moment of distraction, a deer bounding across the road, perhaps. Maybe something sliding off the car seat.

But I also think of those left to grieve. A mother's child is gone ... or a husband or wife, a sister or a brother. Perhaps it was even a grandmother or grandfather.

Whatever, it is a terrible grief, a load we sometimes feel we can't carry another step.

And as I roll past and leave the crosses behind, always there are a couple of lines from an old Roy Acuff song running through my mind:

"Who did you say it was brother?
"Who was it passed by the way?
"I heard the crash on the highway,
"But I didn't hear nobody pray."

It is a mournful dirge, one that brought tears and terrible remembrances to thousands gathered around family firesides on Saturday nights. All the way from the Ryman Auditorium "up there in Nashville," they could see Mr. Acuff's "wreck on the highway" on the radio.

The song was one of Mr. Acuff's major hits and a good guess why is that it touched a tragedy in our lives.

We are, without doubt, fascinated by car wrecks, by tragedy up close.

A hundred thousand can die in a faraway Pacific Ocean tsunami and, for a day or so, the tragedy sort of hangs around us through cable news networks.

"How terrible," we say, even talk about it over coffee for a few minutes. May even mail a check to the Red Cross or Salvation Army.

Then we move on.

But the death of someone we love, or someone we know, in a "wreck on the highway," never leaves our souls.

If the memory, for a little while, takes a break — thankfully, it often does — white crosses by the side of our roads rekindle sadness and hurt and a longing for something no more ... ever.

As I finish this late Saturday afternoon, a gray and misty picture in my window seems fitting ... but there is a need for a confession before I go.

When I started this, there was no intention of it becoming what it has ... if that makes any sense to you.

But those white crosses, this week, that I passed "by the way ... "

T.HE GRACE WITH WHICH
WE LEAVE

JANUARY 6, 2008

Funeral services for Mr. Clifford Lee Vice, age 75, of Wellington, will be Thursday, January 3, 2008, at 11 a.m., at Chapel Hill Funeral Home in Anniston.

— Obituary, January 2

Visitation for Mr. Clifford Lee Vice was the night before. Friends came on a cold, bitter evening to pay respects, to put arms around the wife and say, "If there's anything we can do ..."

There was an open casket and everybody said how good he looked.

One person, arm around his sister, said, "Your brother really was a good-looking man."

All of that is our ritual for going away.

There is another ritual, too, one that comes at the end of a long, long illness. We gather close, in near silence, awaiting the end. Death seems to stand in the shadows, taking its time to "flat-line" the hospital monitor by the bed.

Clifford Lee Vice, age 75, of Wellington ...

He was my brother-in-law and he had, for more years than I remember, suffered from multiple sclerosis.

MS ...

It is a terrible sentence, life and death, too.

Standing in "Suite 306-07" late Sunday, I was again amazed with the grace with which people leave us.

Earlier on Sunday, he still knew his wife of 54 years, Betty Hays Vice.

But somewhere in the afternoon, without whimper or protest, he slipped into unconsciousness. A nurse said, "You need to call family."

At 4:43, the monitor's lines flattened, numbers tumbled, a daughter-in-law knelt and quietly began to switch off the brighter lights in the room.

By his bed were his wife, his two sons, a daughter, two daughters-in-law, his sister.

At the visitation, sitting in the chapel, I watched the people come ... played with memories, including my early days of courting his sister. I'm not sure he was all that fond of the courtship. He had done some courting himself and, well, this was his baby sister ... *NOT* the girl he had loved and married.

Folks, there is a difference.

Then there were the years after he became ill. He finally accepted me after I married his sister, the years he and Betty parented three kids of their own, the years his health declined to a wheelchair, to total dependence on Betty.

And mostly I remembered his good nature, his sometimes silly humor, his acceptance, without whine or complaint, of the hand he'd been dealt.

I sat and watched Betty and it came to me she was the survivor of what had been an unbelievable love affair.

His going was bittersweet ... at best.

But his being here, despite the burdens, the long illness, had been, in fact, pretty good.

In some way, somewhere, I like to think we all contribute, we all enrich the lives around us.

Ties That Bind

I like to think that Clifford Lee Vice, age 75, of Wellington, did just that.

51765908R00102

Made in the USA
Charleston, SC
02 February 2016